Routledge Revivals

Religion, Morals and the Intellect

Originally published in 1932, and therefore inevitably of its time, this book discusses the place of the intellect as a guide to religious truth. The author's work brought principles from Quaker decision-making to bear on wider questions about democracy and religion. The author affirms that the 'Light Within', although a personal endowment is not independent of the historical fact that spiritual geniuses in bygone ages have seen and testified and lived.

Religion, Morals and the Intellect

F.E. Pollard

First published in 1932 by George Allen & Unwin Ltd.

This edition first published in 2024 by Routledge
4 Park Square, Milton Park, Abingdon, Oxon, OX14 4RN
and by Routledge
605 Third Avenue, New York, NY 10158.

Routledge is an imprint of the Taylor & Francis Group, an informa business

© 1932 F.E. Pollard

The right of F.E. Pollard to be identified as the author of this work has been asserted by him in accordance with sections 77 and 78 of the Copyright, Designs and Patents Act 1988.

All rights reserved. No part of this book may be reprinted or reproduced or utilised in any form or by any electronic, mechanical, or other means, now known or hereafter invented, including photocopying and recording, or in any information storage or retrieval system, without permission in writing from the publishers.

ISBN 13: 978-1-032-90336-1 (hbk)
ISBN 13: 978-1-003-55744-9 (ebk)
ISBN 13: 978-1-032-90339-2 (pbk)
Book DOI 10.4324/9781003557449

RELIGION MORALS AND THE INTELLECT

by

F. E. POLLARD, M.A.
AUTHOR OF "WAR AND HUMAN VALUES"

INTRODUCTORY NOTE
by
H. G. WOOD, M.A.

LONDON
GEORGE ALLEN & UNWIN LTD
MUSEUM STREET

FIRST PUBLISHED IN 1932

All rights reserved
PRINTED IN GREAT BRITAIN BY
UNWIN BROTHERS LTD., WOKING

PREFACE

I AM indebted to the Editors of *The Friend* and the *Friends' Quarterly Examiner* for permission to use a few paragraphs here and there which have appeared in their pages. I am grateful to my friends H. G. Wood and the Rev. W. Fearon Halliday for kindly reading these chapters in an early form and for many valuable suggestions; to the Woodbrooke Council for granting me the privilege of a Fellowship for the year 1930–31, during which this book was largely written; and to a discussion group which met more or less regularly during that year, and at which the frank interchange of thought was at once searching and constructive.

I need hardly say that neither the friends named —even though one of them has been good enough to write me an introductory note—nor Woodbrooke as an institution can be regarded as implicated in any of the particular opinions expressed herein.

F. E. P.

INTRODUCTORY NOTE

To young men of my generation, John Morley's book *On Compromise* came as a challenge and a tonic. Many who could not be content with Morley's Positivism, yet owed much to his influence in establishing standards of intellectual honesty and in maintaining faith in the value of conscious critical thought. I must not flatter my friend, the author of this book, by bracketing it with Morley's classic, but readers of the pages that follow will find themselves breathing the same bracing atmosphere as characterizes *On Compromise*.

Our faith in reason needs perpetual renewal. It is imperilled by the narrow view of reason so often held by those who profess and call themselves rationalists. It is imperilled by religious conservatism and timidity, by passions unpurified and undisciplined desires. It is imperilled, strangely enough, in the name of science, by psychologies of the Behaviourist and Freudian types, which belittle conscious intelligence—as if anyone could be a Behaviourist or a Freudian without some conscious intellectual activity! From whatever source the depreciation of reason comes, the reader of this little volume will be forewarned and forearmed against the temptations to intellectual sloth and dishonesty which such depreciation always involves.

H. G. WOOD

CONTENTS

CHAPTER		PAGE
	PREFACE	5
	INTRODUCTORY NOTE	7
I.	THE POINTS AT ISSUE	11
II.	IDEAS OR MEN?	21
III.	REASON AND PROGRESS	30
IV.	EXPLANATION	42
V.	RELIGION A LIFE	54
VI.	FAITH	63
VII.	THE SERVICE OF THE INTELLECT	73
VIII.	THE ARBITRARY AND THE MAGICAL	82
IX.	THE UNITY OF THE MIND	93
X.	THE UNSEEN WORLD	103
XI.	RITES AND SYMBOLS	112
XII.	A RATIONAL MORALITY	123
XIII.	SOME ETHICAL PROBLEMS	134
XIV.	WHAT THEN OF EDUCATION?	147
XV.	A REASONABLE RELIGION	161
	INDEX	181

RELIGION, MORALS, AND THE INTELLECT

I

THE POINTS AT ISSUE

Is the intellect a reliable guide to the most significant truth for men? Or is there a more trustworthy adviser? Thought, feeling, obedience—where lies the clue?

In threading our way through to-day's perplexities of life and thought, it would seem clear that the initial point on which we require assurance, at least if we are wrestling with fundamental things, is this: What function—or may we say faculty?—of the human spirit is it which brings us into closest touch with essential truth? Is there one element in the mind—or one authoritative voice speaking to the mind—which is the sure guide into the heart of things? I put the question thus without prejudice to the nature of the answer, which may very well be that it is no one capacity separable from its fellows that will meet this need, but rather the operative power of the whole mind acting with embracing vision and uniting effect. It is true also that many who feel themselves in the midst of controversies of the deepest import will not recognize this description of the crux of the issue. They are not perturbed by the respective share of different mental elements in the making of truth. They have not asked themselves how they know. They are moved by such problems as the truth of evolution, the destiny of man, the nature of God, the divinity of Christ, the value of Sacraments, the future of marriage, the free development of the individual. There is no question of belittling these themes, but whether they are great or small, are we not, at the risk of academic philosophizing, to ask first what is the instrument of decision? That this query has not arisen in the minds of a particular controversialist does not prove that his conviction is not based upon some assumption as to his ground of certainty. What this assumption is may vary in different cases. It may be the existence of channels of revelation which are considered to carry their own warrant with them; how do they manage this? It may be the inerrancy of human reason; what does this involve? Or others may hold or take for granted that intuition, religious instinct, or some insight born of imagination is able to bring us into immediate touch with reality; are they sure? It would appear, therefore, that the more we enter critically into these problems of religion and conduct, the more we have to examine the nature of the knowing mind. We seem to be driven into the arms of philosophy. As a matter of fact we are all assuming a philosophy. If that is so, had we not better examine its credentials? The simple unquestioning life may let it remain an assumption; but once embark upon the quest, and there is no satisfactory "traveller's rest" at a half-way stage. To vary the metaphor, if we are bent upon shaping the image of truth, shall we not take the preliminary step of assuring ourselves that we have the right instrument for the task?

One difficulty has been—and is still in some measure—that religion has a language of its own. The government of the mind is a dyarchy, if not a heptarchy. Where the head of the religious department is in charge of man's mind, he uses the phraseology of the Creeds and religious writings. He speaks of Christ, the Holy Spirit, the Voice of God, the Light or the Water of Life. He is content with metaphors, which he does not always recognize as metaphors. They may be the right or inevitable messengers of spiritual truth, but it is as well to know their nature; they have certainly been a fruitful source of error. But when the religious representative sits down and another takes the floor, the themes are habits, the association of ideas, effort, ideals, self-control, emotions and sentiments. The conscious life of man may be analysed; the movements of thought and feeling, the decisions of the will, the origin and authority of conscience, may be discussed more or less scientifically. This perhaps is the everyday attitude or the psychological approach, but when again religion enters, the scene changes, and a totally different cast appear upon the stage. This partition into diverse spheres of influence—this duality of language—is as unfortunate as all separatist versions of life and the spirit of man have proved to be. Religion seems outside systematic mental knowledge, and the sciences of the mind often seem to ignore religion except where some abnormalities arrest their attention, or when a whole volume is written on the psychology of religion as clearly a separate subject on its own account. If the religious expressions of reality have been arrived at by some faculty quite other than that thinking power which is used by the scientific investigator or the philosopher, what is that faculty, and what is its warrant? If the religious life of the soul grows on quite different principles from the rest, what are those principles?

It can hardly be denied that this departmentalism is very prevalent, nor surely that it is harmful to have this unresolved opposition, both from the intellectual and the moral point of view. If there is a true departmentalism, it at least requires explanation and defence. However true it may be that religion, morality, and scientific thinking have each their different parts to play in life—and no one wants to obliterate distinctions or reduce the varied enterprises of the soul to one dead level —they are nevertheless all activities of one spirit. It is difficult to think of the supreme qualities of the moral life as other than one with the very meaning of religion, and impossible seriously to imagine that there are two incompatible Truths, one for the physicist and one for the theologian.

It is becoming clearer every day, though there are many quarters into which this has not penetrated, that the impact of the modern mind upon religion is concerned with something far deeper and more far-reaching than the truth or falsity of certain items of belief. The whole question of the sphere, the import and the claims of religion is itself raised in the most fundamental fashion. Those who live in Cathedral Closes may not know it. But it is true. Theological professors may go their way unaffected. But the facts are there. If a Church is mainly agitated by the historicity of Genesis, the existence of heretical views about the Virgin Birth, the legitimacy of reserving the Sacrament, or the burial of Nonconformists in consecrated ground, is it uncharitable to suggest that it is not in a state of growing vitality? You may say that the Churches have to meet the needs not of exceptional free-thinking specialists, but of simple men and women. It may be so, but simple men and women do not always know where their need lies, nor is their simplicity always what others imagine it to be. There is no open discussion of the pulpit's pronouncements. In any case, there are such things as inquiring and troubled minds; it is not pleasure-seeking alone that leads men to absent themselves from public worship; and religious bodies should presumably desire to understand where the danger zone lies, and what are the deepest uncertainties and questionings of thinking men. They claim to be the depositaries of truth: what is truth, and how is it won? They, through their official spokesmen, claim to be the teachers of men: how are their pupils progressing?

May I suggest a few of the radical issues that seem to be involved? We often talk of the head and the heart. Are they two separate organs? Does the head decide some things, and the heart others? Preliminary to that perhaps, does the head see some things, and the heart others? If you can thus isolate thought and feeling, what are their respective spheres? Is there something so analytic and so abstract about the work of the intellect that it is a dangerous guide which can never bring you into contact with the living whole of truth? Is the critical faculty so disintegrating and destructive in its operation that its sphere must be rigidly circumscribed? Is it possible to maintain a practical and working faith whilst leaving the ultimate problems of the universe in suspense? What shall we say to the claim that religion is a matter of life and experience rather than of verbal interpretation or theological dogma? Is a personal devotion to an historical character or to a supreme divine person a *sine qua non*? And, not the least important, must we assert or admit the recognition of the inexplicable as an essential and inevitable element in any devout attitude towards Reality? Must the divine contain an alien ingredient, and is it that which makes it divine? These are religious problems: many ethical ones might be added as to the validity of moral principles; the rivalry of self-expression, discipline and sacrifice; and other urgent matters of vital choice and direction that press upon us.

These queries—or some of them—indicate a tendency to relegate the intellect to a subordinate if not a dubious position, a poor relation of the aristocratic soul, and as a preliminary to our discussion three points of a general character may be noted. In the first place this depreciation of thought may arise from various causes. It may be insufficiently analysed prejudice and suspicion. The undetected cause at work may be that we fear the consequences of thought. Perhaps the psychoanalyst can help us. We have virtually decided where we want to stand, and unchecked thinking may break up the ground beneath our feet. There is also a frequent sense of the unprofitableness of disputation and controversy, as indeed is natural if the conflict is carried on with one narrow edge of the mind regardless of the reserves of broad purposes and conceptions, and if the aim is victory in debate rather than the common effort after truth. A more defensible hesitation may be brought about by a commendable emphasis on practical values; why worry about penetrating the mysterious fastnesses of creeds and dogmas? Or again it may

18 RELIGION, MORALS, AND THE INTELLECT

be based upon a psychological theory of the supremacy of instinct which that vainly pretentious newcomer, reason, must accept without more ado. Lastly it may have its roots in a worship of the mysterious, which requires a special sense for its apprehension, and before which thought is irrelevant.

But it is surely pertinent to urge that in any case this suspicion or subordination is an intellectual act. It is itself a theory, whether deliberately thought out or otherwise; this is the product of the mind as thinker, and as such, however much and however rightly it emphasizes other things than reason, it must run the gauntlet of reason before it can be accepted. A man believes in the Bible: why? Will he dispute our right to ask the question? He believes that what he feels intensely as an experience must imply some direct access to reality. How does he know? Can he convince someone else that it is so? What is his general principle of decision or persuasion? Will he state it and apply it? There may of course be a question—and a very important question—of the most relevant evidence. Have we seen the necessary data, and are we capable of appreciating their significance? Our partial unimaginative minds may be ignoring tracts or fringes of experience which are crucial to the point at issue; but the facts when seen must be coordinated; the necessity of rational adjudication remains. How can a theory cast out theory as such? Satan's ejection of himself is a possibility compared with that! Indeed it is a hopeful feature of the age that men are theorizing, that there is so much general thought playing about ultimate things, even though some of the philosophy sets out to be anti-philosophic!

Secondly, the disrepute of theorizing is partly due to the rejection of particular beliefs which have held sway over the religious mind of the past. We may hold that theology has utterly missed its way, and this is taken as proving that it should not be allowed a right of way at all. The necessity for a re-start is mistaken for a total disqualification. It is true that at times the mind of the Christian Church has been concentrated upon matters which to some seem trivial, remote or meaningless, and that in consequence the simple tidings of the Man of Nazareth have been forgotten, the vital facts of the inward life ignored, and the plain demands of righteousness neglected. Yet science also has a way of revising its opinions. The text books of last year are already out of date. Is it any more reasonable to condemn religious thought because of its errors and misguided emphasis than to reject science because Ptolemaic astronomy or Newtonian physics have been superseded?

Thirdly, this inclination to reject the intellectual, or at least to grant it only an academic interest, suffers from an inherent and vitiating departmentalism. It may be a valuable tendency when it arises from an insistence on quality of life as the one essential. This will demand fuller treatment later. But it may be urged here that it forgets the basic unity of the spirit of man. It leaves out of account—or pigeon-holes (and therefore misses the importance of)—the ineradicable movement of the human mind in the way of seeking and thinking, that endowment which seems to be strangely spoken of by some thinkers as the irrational instinct of rationality, the unreasoning urge to reason. Define religion if you like as an attitude to life or the world. This view is defective if it fails to recognize that our facing of the universe cannot be detached from thought, but is the outcome of impressions and conceptions, coloured with feeling and involving activity. Such a restricted view leaves out the mighty power of ideas. They are not the parochial denizens of one province of the mind. In so far as they exercise their power, they rule the heart as well as the head, and move and direct the will. They *are* the mind, ranging through the universe of space and time, and making of it one thing or another, and comparing it in this or that fashion. Moreover, quality of life is concerned with the use we make of our endowments, and one of these is our capacity to think.

II

IDEAS OR MEN?

Are we right, however, in speaking thus of the power of ideas? It is often said that men are not stirred to enthusiasm by ideas, but by personal loyalty to great leaders. If this is true, or in so far as it is true, it suggests a further reason why the intellect may be regarded from the standpoint of religion as, to say the least, a secondary activity of the spirit. The primary need will then be to arouse an emotional attachment to some impressive and inspiring personality: rational understanding may have its place, but does not help in this chief of all spiritual necessities. It is cold, it does not stir the heart: it deals in "bloodless categories." Is this a sound position?

I am not going to enter here into the psychologist's discussion of the relation of ideation to volition; still less into the ultimate place of personality, human or divine, in the scheme of things. Our problem is one that is simpler and more immediately practical. It is a matter of the most effective ground of appeal—effective in a true and ultimate sense—in the interests of religion. It can hardly be doubted that the right answer is one that takes neither side to the exclusion of the other. That ideas have never moved, and can never move humanity to zeal and new purpose and persistent courage cannot be maintained for a moment. There have been men who died for Protestantism, not for Martin Luther; who suffered for truth, not for Galileo or Darwin; for liberty, not for George Washington or Rousseau. Not for abstractions in the usual derogatory sense. No doubt their thoughts took concrete shape in their minds, and the bearing of their ideas upon the living realities of earth was never forgotten. But that is the way that general ideas are held: they are not suspended *in vacuo*; it is not supposed that they have a life of their own detached from individual facts, events or conditions. But except you fasten upon common features and think them together, you can never think at all.

We need not enter upon the metaphysical controversies as to nominalism or the real existence of general ideas or of forms laid up in Heaven. It is enough that we cannot detect and fasten upon the qualities displayed in particular things or persons without comparison and generalization. We cannot rise from narrowness to breadth of vision unless we can see universal features and hold them before the mind. If it were possible to know only the particular, we should never really know it at all — if the contradiction may be allowed. The same no doubt may be said of universals, but the present plea is not for their existence as separate entities, but as finding meaning in or giving meaning to particulars. Whatever may be said later of the dangers of analysis and abstraction, it is general ideas that lead us to truth, and this applies alike to the knowledge of external nature and to the grasp of moral needs and realities which illumines our judgment, stirs our hearts and directs our wills. There are some who think that philosophy lives permanently in the air, in the rarefied ether of abstract thought, and never gets its feet upon the solid ground. On the contrary, philosophers are just the people who are anxious to know where their feet are. Others do not mind, but they—the thinkers—desire a reliable foundation.

On the other hand, no one will wish to underestimate the added power which is gained when conceptions of life, principles of conduct, convictions as to the relation of man to God, are embodied in the vivid reality of a faithful and glorious life. Such incarnation clothes generalities with life and exhibits them as having their meaning not in "some remoter star" but in the daily living of real human beings. It meets the needs of men not so much by setting up some exemplar to be copied, as by proving that man is capable of reaching the heights—and in the critical moment of choice this is a belief difficult to retain—and by showing that goodness is no melancholy state of privation—and that is what it seems when the enticements of the present are upon us—but a splendid enterprise that attracts and captivates the soul. This power is wielded by every man whose life tells us that courage and loving-kindness and the search for righteousness and truth are abroad in the earth. And the more wholeheartedly and profoundly he has taken them into his being and followed them to the end, however tragic, the more he stirs the deeps in our sluggish hearts and gains our full allegiance and devotion.

All this is true, and if the other side is presented here, it is because the value of thought is our subject and because it has an important bearing upon the right attitude that we should adopt towards the magnetic personalities who are thus marked out as the leaders of men. No such attractive influences can be wholly or reliably healthy if they are accepted in an unintelligent fashion. The real power, or at any rate the real direction, should lie in the understanding and conscious acceptance of the great man's ideas. Otherwise your following of him has become, or remained, a mere animal submission to a dominating force. A man who followed Garibaldi merely from the magical attraction of his personality without grasping in some measure the greatness of his purposes for Italy, was but a poor sort of patriot who might be perverted at any moment by a rival magnet. If devotion to Jesus does not depend at bottom upon a conviction that his vision of life and truth as taught in words and deeds was the most satisfying message ever given to men, Christianity sinks to a mere emotional hero-worship, or a sentimental acceptance of some mysterious external aid. The things he taught are not true because he taught them, as this attitude would imply. He taught them because they are true. Men's worth depends upon their qualities, not the qualities upon the men. Truth and righteousness are greater than their exponents, no matter how perfect the life in which they have been embodied. The life does embody the truth, and righteousness can live only in a person; personality is powerful for truth in that it integrates what might otherwise be left as departmental and partial; it appeals as a whole to the whole in us. But the value lies in the universal reference. The person is sacred, and has intrinsic value, but value is a communal not an isolated fact. What Jesus stood for and was may become an integral part of our very selves, and that is what the living transference of his power to us means.

The excessive or misleading stress thus often laid upon the personality rather than the ideal which actuated it, is bound to tend towards an unprogressive attitude of mind. A literal and slavish attachment takes the place of what might be an intelligent and illumined pursuit of a great purpose. His words stand, and a mechanical acceptance is required. Obedience may follow upon blind devotion. The following of ideals and principles on the other hand, if they are viewed as such,—as guides in the new world that is born every minute,—means growth, adaptation, new vision and understanding. It is the same danger which attends the crudely anthropomorphic representations of God as found in the earlier portions of the Bible. If God appeared in visible shape or spoke with audible voice, how can we, while using this narrative for educational purposes, combine these stories with the conception of the gradual evolution of moral standards or of ideas as to the nature of the Deity? God said this, and there is no getting round the fact, except by explanations which will neither be understood nor remembered. No doubt early instruction in such matters cannot be abstract; it must be illustrative and appeal to the youthful imagination. But the use of the object lesson is to lead to general knowledge; if the concrete example taken is by reason of its primitive character such as to stand in the way of a deeper understanding, you have deliberately erected an obstacle in what is in any case a difficult path to find and follow. This leads to the conclusion that the Old Testament is a perilous handbook of religious education if used, at any rate without wise discrimination, at any age before the evolving insight of Israel or the gradual discipline and revelation of the divine can be viewed as a whole and grasped as a process.

It may be said that the distinctive value of the literature of the Hebrews consists in just this, that it is the product of a wonderfully poetic mind which led them to express the things of the spirit not in dry and bare abstractions or attempts at exact theological statements, but in lyric phrase and the imagery that portrays the deepest and most mysterious facts of the inner life. Or again, the Old Testament is a storehouse of biographical experience and historic narrative where moral and religious truth is "embodied in a tale," or displayed in action—which is just where it should be. Here you may feel is the very thing for the child mind. This is true; but the answer is, I think: first select wisely—there is no poetic and certainly no moral value in a narrative that tells of Jehovah's orders to slaughter all the people of a hostile city. Neither lyrical beauty nor excellence of story-telling must be allowed to condone or cancel out moral barbarity. And second, begin with the known, the inward experience which the child has had and to which these accounts of God's commands refer. When that foundation is laid, and as the power of thought begins to grow, then and then only can these anthropomorphic stories be used without danger to the hopes of a clarified and progressive moral judgment. The appeal of the personal must come in as it can aid and not hinder the capacity to see the universal truth which it enshrines. This has a far wider reference than the education of the young. Are we for instance satisfied to condemn war as incompatible with the teaching and spirit of Christ? This has its right and powerful place when addressed to those to whom it appeals and who understand it; but the personal claim is not the ultimate ground of condemnation, nor will it take effect in many minds which it is desired to reach.

Let me guard myself again from the possible charge of glorifying the abstract, and dismissing the revelation of truth that comes through the vital facts of human history. On the contrary, one of the main points which the foregoing discussion has in mind is that an over-emphasis upon—or a purely emotional handling of—the personal obscures the perception of historical processes; and it is in them that the operative hand of God must be discerned. It is indeed in individual lives and thoughts that this is revealed, but the individual regarded as a revelation is *ipso facto* lifted into the realm of the universal.

It is probable that men will always differ in the degree to which the universal must for them be incarnate in concrete fact or flesh and blood. Even those to whom Jesus Christ is everything are thinking some of them of an inward present friend, others of the Galilean carpenter and prophet. There are minds which are predominantly practical; others are poetic or again analytic or philosophical. But whether the concrete service, the intuitive vision, the imaginative picture, the compelling beauty of a life or the deep meaning of general truths, bulks most largely in the mind, it is fatal to belittle the place of thought. It must always be there; do we want it to be penetrative and sound, or are we content that it remain hazy, uncritical, hidebound, incapable of advance? It is in any case regrettable that those who exalt the place of personality should dogmatically condemn those whose avenue to the highest is by another path. There is no such unbridgeable gulf that one should regard another as a weaker brother, or the other label the one as an unbeliever who has missed the heart of the matter or the gateway to life.

III

REASON AND PROGRESS

IF we are to departmentalize—and we can, of course, safely do so, if we are vigilant in supplying the corrective of a unifying philosophy—let us return to the old idea that reason is the distinguishing quality of man. Our predecessors only erred in cutting off man in his rationality from his fellow animals with their instincts, and therefore from the whole movement of life in the world. There is an unhappy tendency often at work which leads men to glorify by the method of utter separation. Whenever it is desired to exalt the place, it may be, of humanity, or of a certain personality, or of a book, they must needs confer upon it a distinct order of being which effectually isolates it. The Bible, Jesus, divine worship—all these have suffered from this stultifying detachment. The result is that by refusing to bring to bear our faculty of comparison, we miss the intrinsic reasons for admiration and reverence; by locating value mechanically in one spot, the rest of the landscape is shorn of its worth. The consecration of a portion of life in exclusive fashion leaves the rest desecrated. When science or criticism forces comparisons upon us, there is a sense of loss and degradation. When religion broadens out to seven days a week, men fear its dissipation. Yet it is ours to find good in many quarters besides the best and greatest; to identify and fasten upon an element and yet to find it everywhere; to bow before the inspired and the divine, and gain inspiration from them, for the very reason that we find there universal qualities raised to their highest point; to see in man's mental development a stage—the final stage, if you like—in an eternal growth. To trace a continuity from the humblest origins to the loftiest culmination is not to detract from, but to understand in its setting the honour due to the latter; is it not better to have won the heights than to have been deposited there? moreover this has the inestimable advantage that we are enabled to bring all life—perhaps all energy—into a unity of movement, and it may be into a single purposive whole.

All things are influenced by their environment: with mind comes the discovery of meaning in the jostlings of experience, and the consequent opportunity of order and control. Mind, then, may be regarded as that of which the function is as Professor Hobhouse says, "to organize life by the correlation of experiences." In this process of correlation there may be every grade of what we should call in its higher stages understanding or reasoning. The link of point to point may be only felt, or in other words the ground of connection, though operative, is only implicitly present in the contents of consciousness. What this implicit existence really is may be an awkward question, but it is clear that we are here in the presence of an essential feature of mind and its methods of retention and action. At different levels of life, analysis—the making of the links explicit—may be conspicuous by its presence or its absence, or by the limited scope of its operations. To quote the same author again :—

"A chicken avoids a caterpillar because he dislikes the taste. We perhaps refuse to allow that the chicken reasons because he does not know what it is that makes the caterpillar taste bad. After the chicken follows the chemist, who finds that the caterpillar secretes a certain acid. We clap our hands and applaud him as a reasoner who has explained everything. But will the chemist explain why a given acid should have an acrid taste, or show how the experience of unpleasantness should modify subsequent action? A horse learns to lift a latch. We do not think he reasons. He merely has found out how it is done, and does it. A man explains to a child the action of the latch, and shows how by pressing it at one point you lift it out of a catch at another. He, we say, reasons because he analyses the process and how it is done. But a physicist might point out that the man knows nothing whatever about it unless he sees that the principle of the lever is involved in a simple form, and a metaphysician might add that the physicist cannot be said to understand the principle of the lever unless he is prepared to decide whether it is a principle which holds true of reality, and if so, on what epistemological grounds."[1]

The grounds of conclusion or action may then be some merely felt connection between external facts or the broad reaction of the organism as a whole. The fact has impinged upon the mind and played its part in forming it, but the light of consciousness has not been focussed upon it as an independent existence. The course of development will be in the direction of increasing explicitness, resulting in a more or less understood link of causation or, in the case of conduct, a conscious decision of that will, as we call it, which expresses the fiat of the personality.

This correlating power then goes forward with an increasing consciousness of what it is doing, and with increasing attention to detail on the one hand, and scope on the other, till it takes of the instinctive make-up of man, his dim consciousness of common interests, and the social traditions which have dominated his life, and seeks to build up therefrom a coherent scheme of living. Mind becomes at once more defined, more comprehensive, more purposive. Dr. J. E. Turner writes:—

"The evolution of life means the evolution of dominance or effective control of the environ-

[1] *Mind in Evolution*, Macmillan & Co.

ment: this again can be attained only through the evolution of ideation, thought or intellect, as one essential factor or aspect of the increasingly complex, yet at the same time increasingly definite mind: and finally the evolution of mind, when thus regarded in its wholeness as a unified system, culminates in selfhood and personality. Thus Bergson's principle must be substantially modified so that the necessary emphasis falls in its proper place—not simply on Life, but on Thought as the effective factor in life at all its highest levels."[1]

The aim of the present discussion is to find, and if it proves justifiable to exalt, the place of mind in the evolution of life. I need hardly say that there is no pronouncement implied as to whether in this tracing of development anything is being really explained in any ultimate sense, nor whether there do not appear, with all our oneness of process, certain leaps so considerable that we can only call them inexplicable or emergent. Nor are we making any specific assumptions as to the continuity or certainty of human advance, although over an adequate period there can be surely no doubt. Our increase of knowledge is almost painfully evident. In the moral sphere, we are no longer cannibals: we do not burn witches, we only consult them, which if more foolish is less wicked. It is

[1] *Personality and Reality*, George Allen & Unwin.

sufficient here to speak of the progress of life "from the amoeba to the saint," from a colony of protozoa to human society, from a primitive tribe to a modern community of men.

It is urged then that the very instrument and indeed the substance also of progress has been the determination of mind, from its earliest dawn onwards—its essential function indeed—to reduce chaos to order. Mind is the searchlight in the darkness, and the darkness comprehends it sufficiently to reveal its possession of a hidden order or its capacity to submit to and welcome a higher unity. Chaos of impressions passes into a correlated and ordered knowledge, chaos of desires into ordered character, and chaos of individual claims into ordered social life. In this epic, or perhaps we should say prophetic, story, with all that it reveals of the nature of the discerner and of the thing discerned, mind is not to be taken as referring in any isolated way to the cognitive department. It is consciousness in its organic wholeness that is at work, with a unified attitude that in its later stages implies and is made possible by moral feeling and the integration of impulses. Nevertheless the intellect in a broad sense—which is our subject—is an essential if not supreme factor. To see connections and co-ordinations that are or ought to be is to be on the march. In explaining the sense in which even the word intellect is used, there will be no hard-and-fast lines drawn. If some moral elements are introduced as inseparable from the true functioning of the intelligence, that is where they belong; and it is but another testimony to the unity of the spirit. No narrowly ratiocinative meaning is therefore maintained: rather an inclusion of all the capacities and qualities that go to the equipment of the thinker as such. Among them will be alertness of observation; humility in the presence of facts, whether outward or inward; even—what is often thought of as detached from the understanding— a piercing, far-reaching and shaping power of imagination; not to mention a clear controlling purpose, and the saving gift of a synoptic vision. All these are ministers of that ordered mind which takes to pieces with intent to recombine, which is not content with seeking out and analysing, but uses these as the indispensable preliminaries to a richer synthesis. Mind is the great explorer and civilizer; its work is that of peaceful penetration; its goal the larger life.

We are speaking, then, of the realm of knowledge, of the capacity to observe and reflect, to compare, abstract and generalize, the urge to find and make the laws of life. Reason is not destructive; it is not pettifogging; it is not even academic. It is the impulse to harmonize and unify. If it is critical by its essential nature, how else can darkness be illuminated, or discords resolved? The power to turn upon and survey the self and pronounce judgment upon its present stage of ideas and standards is the very hope of humanity. If it deals in concepts, said to be pallid phantoms compared with the flesh and blood of intuition and imagination, these concepts may very well be the indispensable guide to truth, through fastening upon universal qualities or sweeping scattered experiences into integrated wholes. A human being may be abstract compared with a particular Englishman standing before you; but the former has brought the mind to a deeper and wider understanding than the latter, unless the concrete individual is read in the light of universal conceptions. It is the superficial, less important things that divide, the fundamental ones which unite, and the uniting ones which are fundamental. He too who thinks to defend religion by insisting on the personal and the actual in experience is not really shut up in the particular. He does not hesitate to discuss prayer in the abstract; he knows that it has a meaning, a reference, which is concrete enough; but it is through the wider thought that the reality of the individual fact is grasped.

Nor does thought result merely in the naming of large classes of objects or phenomena. It has enabled us, for instance, to gather the incoherent facts of instinctive and conscious life into a more or less ordered and stable self, and from this to form an interpretation of the being of other personalities; or again to rise from a vague sense of a something that binds man to man to some fuller understanding of what society may be and of the meaning of our common humanity. Is there any limit to the advantage that follows when one's thoughts are made more articulate and more comprehensive?

But if rational thought is still considered by some to have led to an arid and superficial view of life and truth, and if there is a measure of foundation for this suspicion, it is not due to any defect inherent in the process. Analysing, combining, testing—there is nothing wrong here; they should bring us into closer touch with reality by fresh groupings, new insight and the ruthless sifting out of error. Even the artist profits by a knowledge of theory. Conscious theory is only a hindering and narrowing influence when it is not only inadequate, but in its arrogant inadequacy obscures some unanalysed vision which in the particular case happens to be truer. If defect there be, it lies in the collection of evidence: has this been sufficient for the occasion? We are especially concerned here with the application of intellect to the sphere of morality and religion. Is it as justifiable here as in the realm of outward nature? "You cannot make a man moral or religious by teaching him about good or about God." No—although there is more to be said than at first appears for the maxim "Virtue is knowledge." Which of us would go astray if we saw things in utter clarity and truth? Our contention, however, is not that the intellect is everything, but that it is of considerable if not major importance.

"But," it may be said, "this pseudo-scientific handling of themes of human character and spiritual qualities fails because it aims at statistical laws, forgets the supreme significance of individuals in all their uniqueness and their richness and variety of content, reduces them to one common and therefore low level, and is probably carried out by those who are in no way sensitive to the most delicate and subtle of the facts in question, and who may be on a moral level at which a true evaluation of the best is impossible."

That this contains an important warning against many current tendencies may be readily admitted. But if it can be taken as implying that because physical science identifies itself with measurement, therefore the name science is inapplicable to that which cannot be measured, I would urge that this is an unjustifiable reduction of its scope. That certain external methods of estimation may be essential for physics is no ground for refusing to apply reasoned thought to the things of the spirit, or for seeking some other instrument of inquiry and judgment. There is none. The idea that the real is the measurable will not stand. But on the latter contention—that important evidence has been ignored—it is true that the preliminary necessity is an ability to see the facts and then weigh them. This is not peculiar to the spiritual realm; the scientist who is too blind to distinguish bacilli under the microscope or to follow the evidence of an electron's path upon the screen, or to detect a line on the spectrum, is as clearly disqualified as the unsympathetic sociologist, the unimaginative critic, or the historian of religion to whom the inner life is a closed book.

There is no need to set sensibility over against science. The necessity of observation plus reasoned interpretation is everywhere. No one will question that the analyst or the classifier, however rational and accurate, may be blind, or neglectful of relevant phenomena. "It is true," writes Professor Alexander, "that Hume himself overlooked in experience facts which were in the language of Plato's *Republic* rolling about before his feet." If the investigator ignores the organic life of the individual whole, he goes astray whether it is in religion or in biology. If in his desire for clear-cut results he rules out all the dim fringes or pervasive elements of conscious life, he may miss the essence of the matter—not because there is some special value in the vague and mysterious, but because here may be just the region where the next advance awaits us, or some factor so involved in the very possibility and meaning of experience as to escape notice. Thought need never divorce us from reality. If it has secured the requisite data—and for this imagination, sympathy, love may be needful—it should by suggestion, illumination and an ordering of knowledge, lead forward to a closer and truer contact with the real. It should go down below the apparent into the depths, find significance where all seemed idle confusion, and see things more truly because they are viewed as factors in the great sum of truth. Reason after all is not an alien, interfering, disputatious judge: it is the human spirit seeking reality.

IV

EXPLANATION

IT is in the broad sense indicated in the foregoing chapter that the word "intellect" is being used in our discussion. It stands for the mind when functioning as seer and thinker, whether enjoying experiences, framing conceptions, discovering facts and uniformities, inventing and testing hypotheses, seeing visions or arriving at moral judgments. It is the power which collects and classifies phenomena, gives form and system to the medley of impressions, constructs purposes and weighs values. Feeling is of course an accompaniment of all these mental processes, and may be of real significance in the matter of valuation. Nevertheless what we may call the substance of the thing is seeing and thinking. Feeling is transient, tidal; the idea outlasts it and is steady. In all this mental activity, there is doubtless an element of dissection, and what may seem cold adjudication; and it is true that it is the mind as critic and judge that is most in need of defence. In taking a broader view, I have no desire to confuse or cover up the issue, but rather to see it in its true perspective. It is only as an inseparable part of a larger whole that the true nature and value of the critical intellect can be understood. We must look at the mind as far as possible as an operative unit,

EXPLANATION

growing in the extent and systematization of its contents, and in the range and clarity of its vision.

It is clear that the hesitation or suspicion which sets out to put a rigid limit to the operations of the intellect or to claim that there are better regions beyond its ken where its writ does not run, springs often from the feeling that when we have achieved what we call the explanation of a fact, we have explained it away. Its pretensions are exploded; we have revealed its illegitimate birth, and dismissed it so that it no longer counts. This notion requires examination. It might have been imagined that the purpose of explanation was to show how things do count, to bring them within our grasp. The function of thought is to get into touch with reality, and it would seem a strange result of contact that the object touched should vanish. Is the knowing relation essentially distorting or destructive? Is it not rather a ministry of service? I am not going to follow up this problem of epistemology, for in the minds of those who cherish this instinctive revolt against the advance of science, it is not a conscious theory of knowledge or agnosticism which is at work, but an impression that the wonder and majesty of the universe diminishes with the progress of explication. A perilous position indeed which is as menacing to religion as it is alien to the thought of the real investigator! It is a poor sort of faith that depends upon or has a preference for ignorance, and a poor sort of science which finds the world divested of wonder in proportion as it is increasingly understood. That some scientists or naturalist philosophers have been so over-confident in their attainment of ultimate truth as to display a world of bare, soulless and uninteresting mechanism is no ground for abandoning the position here set forth.

Some modern theories of the nature of religion lay stress upon the non-rational element in the organ or the object of human worship. Religion is a matter of a special instinct, as if the embracing, unifying power was not of its essence! Or it is suggested that if the nature of God could be understood, He would cease to be revered, we should no longer bow before Him in the humility of "creaturehood." Religion by this account begins with the sense of the weird and uncanny in the primitive mind; and to remain religion it must retain this unintelligible mystery to the end. How far it is right to trace the ancestry of religion as we know it by following the clue of man's emotions is too large a problem to be discussed here. There may be an element of identity or continuity in the feelings with which man reacts to a dream, a shadow, an earthquake or pestilence, a military disaster, a sense of guilt, a sudden revelation or a vision of the sublime. But that this entitles such phenomena, or the mental states engendered by them, to be regarded as the genealogical tree of the best modern conception of the spiritual or of our attitude towards it is not so clear. Dr. Galloway writes:

"Were man a being spiritually complete, or were he doomed to remain for ever unconscious of his own defects, then in neither case would the motives which lead to religion be present."[1] Does not that indicate a different line of descent? But putting that aside, the question must be pressed whether to understand a thing is to cease to be impressed by it. It is said that we only think in abstractions; in all individual things or above all persons, the reality eludes us, a mystery remains that we can never grasp by conceptual thinking—and it is just this mystery which is of supreme importance.

Now if our thinking leads us to a general idea of, for example, criminality and so to classing all criminals together on the basis of some common quality, and if as a consequence we neglect all the special features and characteristics which distinguish particular delinquents, we shall assuredly take a very superficial and mechanical view which misses the heart of the person or the act. But this is not thinking: or at least it is very poor thinking. Comparison and generalization should enable us to understand and judge a concrete case with greater insight, and so to get nearer to reality, not further from it. Professor Whitehead says of man that "general ideas give an understanding of that stream of events which pours through his life, which is his life."

The significant truth of the matter is not that

[1] *The Philosophy of Religion*, T. & T. Clark.

there must always be something unintelligible about the real (if this is true, it proves that our minds, though progressive, are limited in power, not that they are up against something that must always in its essence defy them), nor that this alien element is what saves it from destruction in the act of knowledge. It is rather, firstly, that the reality has an essential unity which thought working through analysis to synthesis can only partially recover. It is true also that, while we know ourselves from the inside, the rest of the universe we know externally: we enjoy the one, we contemplate the other. And thirdly and pre-eminently it is that reality remains something different from our knowledge of it, and will continue to do so no matter how far that knowledge progresses. The more we understand life the better, but we have not thereby possessed it. This though obvious is of the utmost importance, but there is nothing here to suggest any warning to the intellect to keep its activities within bounds or to recognize that they must always be so. There is no reason here why we should regard thought as of an inferior or dubious nature. Nor is the rational so abundant in the earth that we can afford to discourage it.

It is not a question of denying that the unknown vast contributes to our sense of awe; it may even be that the more we learn, the more the uncharted ocean of truth, dimly descried or guessed at, moves us by its mystery. But the ground of awe is not ignorance; it is the felt presence of a mighty reality which we did not and cannot make. Before this we seem small and puny, and our lives poor and ignoble, yet it is a something which is not wholly inaccessible nor without kinship with us—otherwise it would move us not a whit. In its early stages this awe is instinctive; the majesty, whether of the starry heavens or of the moral law, is felt, but not analysed; its meaning is implicit, but not thought out. As understanding advances it should but increase to us the amazingness of the power, the intricacy of the mechanism, the range and subtlety alike of the influences at work, the beauty of the highest reaches of the spirit and the righteousness of its demands. There is no reason why either the analysis of a complex fact or the investigation of the origin of some developed feature of animal or spiritual life should in any way detract from the position they have occupied in our minds. To trace the oak back to the acorn or the human species to the earliest forms of life does not alter the sheer fact of the tree or of the spirit of man. If you have in any sense explained the later stage, it can only be by endowing the beginning with all the potentialities which have ultimately been realized. Omega is never to be explained in terms of alpha; it is omega that shows what alpha had it in it to be. The essence of the matter is shown in the highest that is reached, and that highest stands with all its qualities undimmed. Surely there is nothing here that belittles either the forces that are in operation or the majestic nature of the result.

Seek for the origins of conscience and of the "ought" of the moral law; you may succeed or you may feel obliged to regard it as an inborn bedrock fact of human nature. Even in the former case the important truth remains that human nature is such that it thus develops a sense of moral obligation; the existence and imperative of conscience remain unassailed. The worth of a thing does not depend upon what it was before it had grown. Find the origins of marriage in the most primitive of animal mating, and the true and happy unions that we have known have lost none of their beauty. Rather, if we can trace the evolution of love through countless types and generations, does the universe itself take on a new and fairer aspect. Explain prayer if you like, and the worth of the fact is undiminished. Take the very fact of worth itself, the appreciation of value, the recognition of the sacred; reveal their psychological ingredients, show how they evolved. Not only do they remain in their integrity—man remains such that these things have grown up in him, he has found personality and found it of supreme value—but with this added understanding of their nature and origins, their significance will have become more, not less, impressive. Those who urge otherwise have surely failed to deal in any philosophic spirit with all that a developing reality implies.

It may at times require an effort—a moral, a constructive, an imaginative effort—to turn away from origins and cold analysis to recover our reverence before the integrity of the fact itself; the fact and our attitude towards it revert to a certain simplicity; nevertheless that reverence will be the greater for our fuller knowledge and deeper insight.

It must of course be admitted that this analysis may shatter some old interpretations of the phenomena in question; but the mind has seen a fact, even if its former theory proves defective and requires amendment; and if the inquiry has been sound and thorough and its results pass whatever test reason thinks fit to apply, then we have won a firmer grip of reality—and no one will dispute that that is what we are seeking and needing. Some indeed may feel that this is all somewhat obvious and elementary; but in common thought there is a frequent sense of uneasiness which would be dissipated, if we could once banish the notion that to explain is to explain away, and that religion rests upon the inexplicable. To hold that is to put God in perpetual retreat. He is driven back into the ether, or worse still, the unconscious; He stands or falls with the magical or the miraculous. Perhaps the keys of the situation are to hold fast to facts and not let them be whittled away, and in our mental wrestling to come back from the primary departmentalism of science, and the tendency to think of original sources as explanations of the perfected result of the universe,—to see the world steadily and see it whole, to attain to something of the intuition of God. But this is part of the work of the intellect too—the philosophic reason, if you like, as supplementary to the scientific reason.

Reverence, to repeat the central theme of this discussion, may at first have been ignorant and instinctive; the higher reverence, born of investigation and thought, is incomparably richer.

There is another subject—another aspect of the life of the spirit—which may be included in this section: and that is spiritual guidance. There are times when the perplexities that beset us, the alternative courses that present themselves to us, are best resolved or decided upon, not by an explicit tabulation of the issues and a conscious and deliberate reasoning from the premises, but by quiet waiting for guidance. Here the condition of attainment is not intellectual skill but the possession of a sensitive spirit ready to hear and ready to obey. We do not seem to be agents, but recipients. Men whose souls are thus attuned find the path of duty made plain. Meetings which fall into silent waiting, in withdrawal from distracting voices and in the expectation that light will be vouchsafed and the way of progress and unity open out before them, are not disappointed. Are we to say that here we are in contact with a higher faculty than reason for the attainment of truth? that here is a spiritual sense, which is distinct from normal mental powers, and which gives access to spiritual truth beyond the range of ordinary effort? I am only concerned to touch this question so far as to urge that if we can in any sense explain this kind of experience, or bring it into line with other phenomena or processes of the mind, we shall not in the least diminish its value in itself or its significance for a spiritual interpretation of the universe. The sense of recipience occurs along many other avenues of thought and feeling. Perhaps it would be true to say that the more we look into any facts of consciousness the more certain we are to find this element. The poet, the artist, the inductive scientist —to each his inspiration comes; he does not concoct it. He may be able to trace the introductory steps which led up to it, or he may not. Does it matter? does it affect the value of the result? does it even affect the fact of its newness and givenness?

It is true in many spheres besides that of critical decisions or the calls of duty that the best mode of reaching a sound conclusion is to hold all the data in the mind and leave them as it were to sift out the truth: or you may carry through the detailed steps involved in mental or physical action most securely by fixing attention upon the purpose or the goal and letting the process take care of itself.

There are remarkable instances—I am most

familiar with them in the annals of the Society of Friends—of those who have felt guided—compelled one might say—to do apparently irrational and purposeless things, who have obeyed the call, and learnt afterwards of the service they had rendered to some one in dire need. It must have needed an overwhelming sense of the compelling summons to lead a man to preach in an empty house; he knew no reason for it, but there was someone there unseen who heard and went away a different being. Such cases have been by no means infrequent, and there is no ground for doubting the truth of the narratives. Can we explain these? I am not going to claim any such power. Nevertheless, we may remind ourselves that many insignificant facts fall upon the mind without being singled out for notice, which nevertheless play their part in producing an ultimate impression, opinion or resolution. We sum up a situation or make a preliminary estimate of character where the evidence is implicit but has never been analysed out and brought into the focus of consciousness. This kind of process leads to many results which we should be hard put to it to defend by specific arguments. Are such remarkable if not miraculous incidents as that alluded to above explicable on these lines? I am content to urge that even if they are, there is nothing lost. To rest the significance of the case upon its unexplainable quality is to banish all obedience to duty based upon conscious thought and understood evidence to a lower plane: there is no virtue in a lack of understanding. If we want evidence of divine guidance, let us find it in the thought that leads to considered action as well as in the following of unknown clues.

V

RELIGION A LIFE

It has now been admitted, you may urge, that the essence of the matter is one of moral attitude, not at all of intellectual acumen or correct logic. Let it be so: the contention put forward here is not that critical understanding is everything, but that it helps. Moreover, if the phrase "moral attitude" is taken as having a purely emotional connotation, or as referring to volitional activity, or to the two together to the exclusion of understanding, we are again forgetting the unity of the mind. Does the cherishing of the right emotion depend upon an unintelligent attitude towards its object? Is it better to have a purpose without understanding it? Is it possible indeed to set an end before ourselves without the exercise of reason? How else except by the power of thought can we be liberated from the bondage of the present? Is there any chance of finding purpose in life and the universe, without thinking about it? Nor is it any more true in this case than in any other, that it is a matter of moral attitude. Thought and action are not two distinct things. In thought the mind is in action; a moral attitude is involved in all activity, and this includes not only what we call practical life, but equally the efforts of the intelligent and inquiring mind. The value of thought depends upon its purposeful and devoted direction.

What is true is that in the process of critical analysis or the inquiry into origins, some religious dogmas will have to be transformed; and the change may be, in the first instance at any rate, from metaphysical assertions into requirements of a certain moral attitude towards the universe. Instead of assenting, or asking for assent, to the statement that "all things are for the best," we shall be prepared to say "I am capable of wresting good from any thing"; or shall we go further and say that the thing and I—or the universe and I—are such that I can wrest good from it if I will? Plato makes one of the most tremendous statements ever uttered, when he says "No evil can happen to the good man." This relates primarily to the meaning of evil and good, with a stress too upon the word "happen." But it may be taken also as an assertion of the kind of universe we live in. So, setting out to define an ethical position, we find ourselves —perhaps unexpectedly—saying something about reality. Again, theology's declarations about Christ's person may have to be replaced by an appreciation of His character and the nature of His mission and His power. But to make this transformation is an intellectual act, and to revere we must needs sit still and learn. Once more reverence is enriched by thought: thus it finds the true momentous issue, thus it fastens upon the real point of greatness.

The relegation of intellectual statements of belief to a secondary, dubious or unnecessary place owing to insistence on the supremacy of the practical ideal —the claim that religion is life, not creed—demands some further consideration. It is so true and so important that one hesitates to criticize it. In many quarters it would seem the one thing to insist upon. Religion, not departmental, not verbal, not dogmatic, but at the heart of life and embracing all in its sweep: God in the very texture of the spirit: what is more urgent for understanding acceptance to-day? Yet the necessity of intellectual justification remains—not to mention all the other gains that thought and a living mind can bring to the spiritual life. Without it there is no defence against the questioner, whether our own doubting self or another. Without it there is no line of advance to inner clarification, no means of fortifying the soul by elevating personal experience in which only narrowness and self-satisfied ignorance can feel confidence, into universal truth with the sense of security and community which it brings. There is still the need of stamping the inner conviction with the seal of common validity, so that we may be not only well founded upon the rock, but in a position to join with others in an effort after the truth which is both theirs and ours. How far it may be possible to find this foundation without making the leap from inward fact to celestial metaphysics is another matter. Perhaps the answer is that all this involves a metaphysic, and we cannot escape the need of one; or that the worship of the future will not be, as that of the past has so often been, centred emotionally upon detached and self-sufficient beings —a magnified non-natural man seated upon the circle of the heavens—but upon eternal values, wherein personality finds its truest life. Or we may come to assure ourselves that values and purposes are unintelligible apart from a universe which finds its unity and end in a single supreme consciousness.

But in any case it is essential to disentangle the problem as we have viewed it from that of the acceptance of creeds. A creed is static, and tends to be regarded as obligatory irrespective of personal assurance and verification. That conception must go, and it is better that it should go avowedly than surreptitiously; and if its departure breaks the ground of much supposed religious agreement, or dooms to failure some efforts after a union of the Churches, we must face the consequences, remember the gain in intelligence and sincerity, and seek other modes of unity. This is not to cut ourselves adrift from the heritage of the past, nor to lose our regard for and sense of indebtedness to those who have seen more deeply into truth than we, unaided, could ever hope to do. But it is to take of the experience of others, and by understanding it to make it a stimulus and enlargement to our own, and not a substitute for it.

An approach to religion which is to some extent akin to this identification of it with life, is that which emphasizes its relation to poetry and art in its methods of expression. Matthew Arnold, for example, contrasts the abstruse dogmas of certain creeds, as enunciated by certain bishops—so abstract and remote, so unconnected with life and any real knowledge—with the attitude of the Hebrews as expressed in the lyric language of the Old Testament. Here in the Psalms or prophetic poetry are no metaphysical subtleties about the triune Godhead, but imaginative phrases, bold symbolisms and figures of speech, thrown out in the effort to bring the truth home to other men's minds, and to embody the writer's own emotions in confronting the glory of the mysterious power that makes for righteousness. Are we then to look always for the figurative, the concrete imaginings, and to shun the intellect's abstractions and exactitudes, in order to keep religion in touch with life?

Mr. Lawrence Hyde writes that "the truth about human beings and their relationships can never be stated in words; it can only be revealed, shown."[1] Imagination is to mediate between religion and rationality. According to Mr. R. G. Collingwood, "religion can never say what it means," it "claims truth, but refuses to argue"; if the higher religions succeed in expelling the forms and conventions which they have inherited, it will be "at the cost

[1] *The Learned Knife*, Gerald Howe.

of ceasing to be in any recognizable sense religions and becoming philosophies."[1]

Dr. Temple dwells in one of his addresses upon the contrast between science and poetry. Science views things externally, is concerned to break up the object and study its component factors, lives essentially in the eternal restlessness of the mind, soon grows out of date, and is itself moving further and further away from the ordinary man's way of looking at things. Poetry and Art, on the other hand, make us see the thing concrete, alive it may be, and whole, create in us a peace of mind as the inmost truth in its unity sinks into the soul, and lift us above the changing flux of things into the region of the eternal: the fulfilment of this is to be found in worship and religion.

To quote Mr. Collingwood again, "God is the imaginative and intuitive form in which the absolute reveals itself to the religious consciousness."

The place of imagination has been already touched upon, and the preference of the human mind, at any rate at certain stages, for the concrete rather than the abstract, will arise in a later connection. Nevertheless, if the views just presented can be rightly taken, as it seems to me they can, as an attempt to withdraw religion from the jurisdiction of the rational, or at least to minimize or dismiss reason's aid in reaching or expressing the truth of religion, and this in the alleged interest of

[1] *Speculum Mentis*, Oxford Press.

its place and power in life, they demand consideration here, and a few points may be tentatively put forward in comment thereon.

There will be no thought of questioning the contribution made by imagination, either to religion or any other aspect or sphere of knowledge; is not imagination indeed a pictorial mode of thinking, which must find and make good its place in the whole strategy of the mind? Nor will any wise rationalist dispute the value of poetry as a vehicle of profound truth, or the significance of any other art—music, for instance—as a revealer of secrets which it may be can be reached in no other way, and possibly can never be expressed in words. Professor Hocking calls poetry the playground of ideas, in contrast to philosophy their hard-labour-ground: and a playground is a place of education as much as the classroom. A detailed criticism of the views in question might indeed detect some difficulties and objections. As has already been urged, there is no reason why we should confine "science" to that which deals with objects externally. This is a dogmatic limitation of the term which is responsible for endless—and needless—perplexity and harm. Part indeed of Mr. Hyde's case may be taken as a polemic against these restricted claims. The internal enjoyments of the mind, although they may present serious difficulties, are legitimate material for that rational thinking which seeks to coordinate and interpret the facts of the world—

and that process is science. It is also worth repeating that human reason is not content with analysis: its work is to grasp reality. If science does not cover this, then philosophy must come in to complete the work; but indeed the partition between the two is wearing thin. Imaginative constructions and inspirations are indeed potent instruments which the reason uses in its progressive task of bringing light into dark places and order into chaos, and uses in natural science as truly as anywhere else. But having played its pioneer part in pushing forward the boundaries of knowledge, imagination will submit its claims to the arbitrament of reason. If in the sphere of inner experience, imagination clothes the facts—which have been or are at the moment felt rather than identified—with the garments of vivid imagery or the flesh and blood of personal life, this may serve one stage of human development, some needs at all stages, to admirable purpose. But the time will come when these constructions will have to run the gauntlet of rational judgment. If reason should decide that their service to human needs is a guarantee of their truth, then their presentation of the case will stand, but it will stand because reason has so judged. It is a perilous policy to pin your faith to anything which seeks to defy or supersede reason. She has a way of getting the last word.

No one is proposing to assert that the object of our worship is identical with our reasoned statement about it, any more than that the Milky Way is identical with astronomers' opinions about it. But our "attitude" towards the Milky Way—if we have one—is presumably dependent upon knowledge. Thought, in so far as it succeeds, takes us to the heart of things. If worship is a renewal of the sense of the worth of life, it can only be helped by added understanding. If religion can only maintain herself by refusing to argue, then she is in an uncomfortable plight, and philosophy will have to get on without her. I hesitate indeed to draw this distinction at all. The Stoics failed ultimately to meet the religious needs of men, not because they preached a philosophy, but because they preached an inadequate philosophy. As a matter of fact, religion does argue: she explains herself in theology, and theology depends upon a philosophy which it either works out or assumes. The claims of religion can never be detached from the necessities of judgment, nor can she do otherwise than gain by such exposition of her contents and meaning. Not even the messages of Æschylus or Keats or Beethoven can claim exemption from Reason's summons to the witness-box. Joyful acceptance is a different thing from cross-examination, but it cannot dispense with it. It is the truth we want, and the expansion and exhilaration of mind that comes with its embrace.

VI

FAITH

THE challenge to reason has most commonly been thrown down in the name of faith. It is this particular opposition which has been conspicuous in most of the conflicts between religion and its rationalist critics. Following the author of the Epistle to the Hebrews and his successors, and in spite of Paul's declaration that "the greatest of these is love," faith has been regarded as the pre-eminent Christian possession. But what is faith? Its meaning has been by no means a fixture. From the apparent divergence of Paul and James onwards, the word has had various interpretations. But these fall broadly into two classes: one in which faith is a faculty of mind transcending, if not overriding, reason in the apprehension of religious truth; in the other it is a moral quality essential for the maintenance of the good life. It need hardly be said that there is no hard and fast line between the two types; the shades of meaning that appeal to different thinkers and prophets are infinite. The degree of distinction will indeed depend upon how closely religious truth is felt to be bound up with the moral quality of life, or how far it lives in a remote and metaphysical region of its own.

Take first then the moral meaning. If we can

establish that as a fact, can show that in some vital sense faith is a thing of power in the spiritual life, we shall perhaps feel less perturbed if its place in theory should prove dubious, unconvincing or hard to define.

If we examine the famous list of heroes of faith which the Epistle to the Hebrews gives us, do we feel constrained to ask what common quality is exhibited by this heterogeneous collection of men and women? If we have put no such question, is it not rather strange? If we have been content to say "faith in God," are we in danger of bondage to words? God is not an external person so that any reference to Him by name is unmistakable. What is there that concerns us in the conviction of a Jericho prostitute that the tribal God of the raiding Israelites would lead them to victory? Clearly there is no common theological belief among these people; there is not even a common respectability. In what sense then can they be regarded as shining exemplars of faith? In this, that in very diverse fashion they thought they saw which was the Lord's side—varying in meaning perhaps from an anticipation of victory to a genuine perception of good and right—and seeing it, held fast to their convictions in spite of every temptation to the contrary. It would seem to have been a combination of insight and courage—insight that could see beneath the superficial, the transient and the apparent to the deep, the abiding and the real, and courage to keep their vision before the mind and follow it unflinchingly, no matter what allurements of ease or threat of suffering might tempt them to another path. It is very like Plato's "courage," a kind of safekeeping of the true opinion as to what kind of things are to be feared and what not feared, a fast dye which no lye of pleasure or pain will wash out.

It may bring out the essence of the matter according to this interpretation, if the list be extended to those of other races and faiths and of more recent date.

By faith Euripides, in writing *The Trojan Women*, though dealing with the national epic and writing when his city was engaged in a desperate struggle, put aside the glamour and the glory and revealed the miserable issue of war in all its human tragedy.

By faith Socrates, when offered a way of escape if he would promise to abandon his appointed task of summoning his countrymen to wisdom and virtue, was enabled to say to his judges, "I must obey God rather than you."

By faith Alfred the Great resisted the temptation to unlimited warfare, saw the needs of his subjects and set himself to meet them.

By faith Francis of Assisi in setting out to serve mankind, abandoned all that seemed to make for security and even influence, trusted to an unhampered life of sympathy and love to the uttermost, and delivered and followed the message of his Master.

By faith John Woolman cared not for worldly success, rose triumphant over his own shrinking nature, and laboured patiently and humbly with his fellow-Friends and others in the cause of African freedom.

By faith John Bright, when in the high tide of popularity as the tribune of the people, was steadfast in his opposition to the Crimean War, though it meant isolation and such a loss of favour that he was burnt in effigy in his own constituency.

These are samples, and that they are all prominent men is accidental: the same qualities of insight and faithfulness could be found in countless obscure lives, and in the facing of humble and unexpected tasks. Note also that their ultimate justification, though plain to us, cannot have seemed so to them: it was a moral certainty of good, not a demonstrable vision of achievement, that carried them through.

The instances chosen are all concerned with great moral issues. Perhaps we should gain a still wider view of the potency and meaning of faith, if we added that by faith Columbus held undaunted on his way across the Atlantic, though the peril from mutinous crews was great and the prospects of his enterprise seemed desperate. Giordano Bruno and many others in realms of thought and action which we do not usually label as moral, could be added to the list.

There is nothing that clashes with reason in all this. We are in the sphere of activity rather than theory, of conscience and will, of moral sensitiveness and determined faithfulness. Thought is not absent—how could it be?—but there is no antagonism between the dictates of faith and those of thought. Only the occasional misguided identification of reason with selfishness could imagine otherwise.

But there is the other type of meaning which implies that faith gives a guarantee to theories—it may be of the spiritual order and governance of the universe—which reason cannot give and against which it may even protest. Without discussing the various forms which this antithesis has taken, in the hands of the fathers or scholastic philosophers of the Christian Church, one may take the above as a broad statement of the position, and discuss it briefly in its bearing upon the place of reason in religion. Sometimes the claim for faith approximates to that for imagination, which reaches forth beyond the limits which reason strictly speaking has established. It is the advanced guard of reason, the exploring party. If so, as we have seen, it may render good service, but its work must be confirmed.

Sometimes again the faith claim seems equivalent to the assertion that the heart has its reasons which the head can never know, that the heart rises in wrath and answers "I have felt." What shall we say to these statements? This at least, that if the head does not know the reasons (and it is noteworthy and indeed strange that they are "reasons"!), it must be informed, and then it will pronounce judgment. But indeed this dualist metaphor is very misleading, and all the more so because of the ambiguity of the term "feeling." To trust to having felt has nothing to do with emotion, but means that unanalysed convictions are in certain cases to be liberated from the necessity of examination, for their assertions are beyond question. But why? All these claims for faith demand an answer to that question: in so far as we are beings with freely acting minds we are compelled to put it. If reason is satisfied with the answer, then she will add her imprimatur. The case is not dissimilar to the position that there are some truths which can only be proved by living them out. Very good: first you feel that you have a grip upon what is good, and you act upon this unanalysed assurance; then if living by this faith is the test that reason applies, let it be applied sincerely and wholeheartedly. Reach out into the unknown, frame your hypothesis—though you may not put it that way—test it faithfully and to the uttermost, and abide by the result. But do not distrust or depreciate reason. She is the handmaid of truth. As a great unifying power she is a minister of religion.

There are two other points to be noted. Faith, it is said, is a virtue, to exercise faith is a duty. How can it ever be a duty to use the will in order to maintain a belief without regard to the cogency of the evidence? Is there a sense in which this is rationally defensible? It is certainly a doctrine which has often proved dangerous, subversive of reason, hostile to any real desire for truth. To maintain it, some rely upon the weight of authority which dispenses with individual judgment and is therefore an influence which degrades the status of manhood. Others foster the supposed virtue of tame acceptance in a flood of emotion which overwhelms doubts, and clouds and mystifies the light of the mind. Such a method can only commend itself to those who, if one is to judge by their acts, prefer mental obscurity to enlightenment. The view that an act of faith lies at the basis of all knowledge is another matter, and will be touched on shortly.

The truth contained in this thought of faith as an obligation, a duty to crush and hold down irreligious doubts, lies here: we may easily lose or surrender our grip upon essential truths, not for any intellectual reasons, not because of any new evidence to the contrary or any hesitation as to the value of the old grounds of belief, but by reason of moral deficiency or laxity. Here then we are back again with something very like our first type of faith, which as we saw involved insight together with safe-keeping. We are only extending its scope in the direction of theory, and the theories we are talking about have a close relation to life. Sloth, indolence, a preference for the easy course, a tendency to drift with the stream, a desire, hardly conscious, to gain position and play a fine part among our fellows in a line of action that is popular—all these things may tempt us to relegate our true beliefs to seclusion, to hide them away, to let them slip, to hold them as theories which will not bear the test of practice (as though a theory could be true which will not work). Here the will, the insistent expression of the mind's united judgment, may well be brought in to defend the pass. "I do believe, I will believe." But how much more ready and able we shall be thus to call up our reserves, if the conviction in question—the citadel to be defended—is of our own personal building—born (to drop the military metaphor) of our own inquiry, and grasped by our own understanding!

The other point to be noted is this, and it is a philosophical consideration on which there is no necessity to dwell at length. It may be argued that all our religious beliefs, however rational, depend upon certain fundamental acceptances, *a priori* truths, the holding of which is not a matter of understanding or reasoning from evidence, but of faith. Others would meet this by adding that the whole structure of scientific knowledge rests equally upon unproven assumptions. Can you demonstrate the reliability of the universe until you know it wholly? If such a critique of experience is accepted (and there is much to be said for regarding religious truth and natural science as resting upon the same assumptions) it is of profound importance; but once more there is nothing here to shake our allegiance to reason. We have but dissected the nature of the experiencing and ordering mind. We have dug down o its basis, and that must be ascertained to be a sound foundation. No assumptions will continue to be held unless their place is progressively justified, and it matters not whether the test is one of inductive argument, of transcendental criticism, or of pragmatic value. Such an attitude may affect our ultimate metaphysic, may rule out some Absolute or Naturalist philosophies; but it will not affect our estimate of reason's place in the attainment of truth.

In concluding this examination of the place and meaning of faith, I would ask the reader not to impute to the writer any desire to neglect or make light of that borderland of experience and intuition which is perhaps dim and confused; the mind as a sensitive whole is conscious of the import and pressure of these things, but finds it hard to bring them into the focus of full consciousness. Drag them into the light, and their reality seems to fade. Try to express them in rational language, and something of their essence and significance has vanished. It should not be so: there is no reason why the rational mind should be hard and dry, nor light be destructive of beauty. But if faith by its hold on the elements of worth can help us here, we shall not wish to disavow or discard its aid. The problem is to find the best instrument of vision. Reason is not above vision and experience; it desires to see the facts, including those on the very confines of conscious experience, and those ingredients so deep and universal that they pass unnoticed. It desires to collate and interpret these facts, and so to minister to the needs of life. It is the servant of good. The facts and their values are given; they are found and appreciated by the insight of the seeking and thinking spirit, and held fast by its tenacious faith.

This very faith which clings to the reality of unseen factors such as the superficial mind cannot hold, is aided by that intellectual survey which reveals in History the power of "the things that are not to bring to nought the things that are."

> The Cæsars and the Alexanders pass:
> While he that drank the hemlock, he that drank
> The cup more dread on Calvary's hill, remain,
> Servants and mighty conquerors of the world.

VII

THE SERVICE OF THE INTELLECT

ONE cannot help wondering at times whether there is something inherently absurd about this whole discussion. Why should the mind solemnly consider whether it itself is any use in the world? How indeed can it do so? Or perhaps the truth is that here is just the most notable feature of the case, that mind is a mirror that can be turned in any direction, even into itself, and appraisingly upon itself! However that may be, we are going to consider the services of the intellect, both in the past and the future, what the intellect has done, and what we may ask it to do. If we appreciate the past, we shall have a surer understanding of the needs of the present and future, and of the best hope of ministration to those needs. The personal debt which we owe to the intellect, to thought—the debt, that is, relevant to our present subject, over and above the external utilities which science has provided, or the place of mind in the whole process of evolution—deserves some further statement, although it is obvious that no detailed account need or can be given.

Think first of the overthrow of error, and think of it not just in a fighting spirit, but grasp the inner meaning of the task. This, negative and destructive though it may seem, has meant something very positive. The distinction of negative and positive is often indeed a matter of words and method of approach; at times "negative" becomes a mere unmeaning term of abuse. The clearing away of obstacles carried with it a freedom of passage; if we affirm the existence of creative life, what better service is there than to release it?

Mr. Collingwood writes:—

> "The material utility of science, its service in feeding and clothing and sheltering us, carrying us from place to place and providing us with comforts, is the least part of its importance. Its real gift is simply the end of dreaming and the promise of a waking life. It sweeps aside with a ruthless hand all mythology, all symbols that are heavy with unrealized meanings, and dark with the terrors of dreamland, and bids the mind face the world's mystery armed with nothing but its five senses and the sling of its wit."[1]

Whether this is an adequate account of its method and resources depends perhaps upon the nature of the pebbles in the sling!

Reason has brought nature without into such degree of ordered and manageable knowledge, and nature within under such control of principle, as we have attained. All this—and how much of human

[1] *Speculum Mentis*, Oxford Press.

progress it includes—is due to the upward pressure and the expanding influence and scope of what we may call the Universal Reason in man, dim at first, but growing in clarity and command, as man has been responsive and faithful. Reason has meant the increasing capacity to set conscious aims and organic conceptions before us, and so to make possible—however far to seek it still is—the purposeful ordering of life. Science has given us a far more spacious and majestic universe than our forefathers knew, a universe which for all its formidableness is a less terrifying one, and for all its alien and inhuman forces is more friendly and more open to control in man's service. From her disciples, religion has learnt, or if she has not, she has had the chance of learning, to add the love and disinterested service of truth, the spirit of tolerance, and other excellences of intellectual integrity and devotion, to her list of virtues. Nor indeed is there any need to argue from the sum of specific benefits. Are our native endowments gifts of God which are meant to be developed and used? The exercise of the intellect is itself a great activity of human nature whose free functioning should be fostered by any religion worthy of the name. Even from what we call the spiritual point of view, who does not know, if he thinks about it, the inner value to be gained from the intellectual mastery of some branch of thought or knowledge, be it small or great? The muscles of the mind become more fit; the sense of the worth of life—

of his own life—is deepened; he goes forward with a new hope, a new self-respect too which, if combined with humility, as it may very well be, is healthy and stimulating. He has desired freedom, and finds that mastery is one of the keys to it. Full development of potentialities and the setting of them in an all-embracing unity of personality are surely part at least of the essential mission of such a religion as can be honoured to-day.

To all this might be added much that would tell of the application of reasoned knowledge to religious records, intellect weeding out the tares and making the wheat live again. The developments of Biblical Criticism have given the Jewish and Christian Scriptures a new and vivid interest. Hebrew religion has leapt into life because we have seen it growing. A reverence that would not investigate has given place to an infinitely finer attitude of mind which has so deep a regard that it is determined to know. The timidity that guarded like a gaoler has been exchanged for a courage that seeks a close and understanding contact. A concentration of study upon the Gospel records has both implied and kindled a fresh desire to see Jesus as he was, and to understand the substance and spirit of his teaching. If the results of research and debate leave many points in doubt, it is certain nevertheless that it is an unspeakable gain to have brought these things into the setting of history and the light of intelligent consideration, instead of leaving them detached, isolated, arbitrary in their claims, and depending for validity upon their own assertions and upon the very miraculous element which they contain and which is one of the grounds of doubt.

With the foregoing brief statement of a great contribution, we pass to the services, on the same lines, meeting new needs, which thought may render in our own day. Lord Morley once said that the roots of mischief for historians and politicians were looseness of mind and narrowness of vision. But why limit the diagnosis? The same is true of all of us, and assuredly of the Churches, the man in the pew and the man in the pulpit. In these latter cases it takes the particular form of a preference for the sentimental which suffuses reason almost to the degree of submergence, the arbitrary which is oblivious of or superior to rational considerations, and the magical which is incapable of conceiving the value of intelligence or the meaning of causal sequence. But facts with their intrinsic worth and meaning and the demands they make for rational handling will not be denied. So will men be constrained more and more unreservedly to recognize the intellect both in the broader and more restricted sense as a servant of the joint interests of thought and life. Reason will be seen as the arbiter or artificer who takes of the things of experience and gives them back to man in a form suited to his service, who fastens on their implications, reveals their setting in the pattern of life, and enables man to discover, develop and apply the laws of progress and well-being.

It is plain that the prospective services of the intellect are as far-flung as life itself: but it may be possible to select some lines of such service which are particularly called for to-day in the cause of religion and conduct. A brief statement here may serve as introductory to a fuller treatment in succeeding chapters. Firstly, the defence of a truly spiritual religion. This means a warfare against the insidious relics of magic and superstition which abound, and the present bewildering tendency to devise and follow new forms of sorcery, unreason, and all the unmeaning irrelevancies of the occult. It means also an effort to combat, or amend in a spiritual sense, such external conceptions of the meaning and contact of the human and divine as reduce inspiration, revelation, the summoning and redemptive power of God, to something capricious and yet in a sense mechanical, an alien irruption into human life, like the switching on of an electric current or the injection of an anti-toxin.

Secondly, the development of a true psychology, which, while making full use of the added modern understanding of instinct, self-activity, suggestion, sublimation and the distortions due to unremembered shocks and strains, will reassert the unity of the mind's life and reinstate ideals and conscious purposes in their supreme place as the growing points of the spirit of man. Religion, which itself aims at the evocation of the combined and harmonized life of the soul, is more deeply concerned with this than with many much debated effects of modern psychology upon items of Christian belief.

Thirdly, the leading of men generally to a belief in the reality and power of the unseen world, not as semi-material or a shadowy replica of outward things or a congregation of celestial beings which better eyesight would detect, but as the realm of the supreme values and their revelation through and their impact upon individual lives. Are ideals real? or do we prefer ghosts?

And fourthly, and by no means of least importance, the rehabilitation of morality, and the replacement of its undermined and crumbled basis of authority by an intrinsic, natural and rational foundation. The element of authority will remain, but it will be "in thy mouth and in thy heart"; and reason will defend and direct it.

A further point may be added here as to an urgent need, though it is one which is to be met not so much by any fresh intellectual effort as by a willingness of religion in its organized capacity to accept and use the results of modern scholarship. The situation is a strange one. Knowledge grows, but practice lingers. Biblical Criticism—we have already dwelt upon the point—has achieved great results in bringing a breath of new and living reality into the Hebrew and Gospel stories: and in spite of all uncertainties and differences of opinion, has established the soundness of its methods of approach and a large body of definite conclusions. Yet the Christian Churches, even those whose ministers in large numbers accept this criticism, go on their way in all the instituted portion of their services totally oblivious to it. The readings from the Bible, the phrases of the Creeds, the language of set prayers and repetitions, the choice of hymns, the observance of rites, even the phraseology of sermons and extempore prayers,—all these things proceed as though the last century of thought had never been. The unintelligent acceptance of the past and its consequent momentum carries the old order along with it. Those who have enlightenment exhibit a hesitation and caution that amounts to timidity, or perhaps are content to remain an illuminated few while the older views do very well for the many.

Consider for example the birth stories of Jesus. It needs no Higher Criticism, but only a little free working of the mind and a measure of honesty, to see the patent facts, which no sentiment, however beautiful, should be allowed to cover up. Two of our four narratives say nothing about these stories: the other two, while recounting many incidents, agree in no single respect except the mere fact of the birth at Bethlehem and the subsequent residence at Nazareth, and in some points are totally irreconcilable. The attempts to harmonize them with one another or with the facts of Roman history

—whether in regard to the genealogies of Joseph, the methods of the Roman census, the shepherds and the wise men, the behaviour of Herod or the reason for going to Nazareth—are more ingenious than either commendable or successful. Can these things be relegated to the writings of critics, and ignored by the Churches? Do we want the truth? or do we prefer the old ways and a comfortable unperturbed life therein? This is but one sample of a much greater need—the need that organized religion should welcome intelligence, and use it with sincerity. There have been many who have been possessed of the modern spirit at its best, and who have been shining examples of dedicated scholarship, from Erasmus onwards. But has the Church listened to them? Does the Revised Prayer Book suggest it? Do the accepted Creeds—the simplest of them—stand unaffected? If the old language enshrines profound spiritual truths which are vital for man's well-being, and which could never have survived without the aid of unspiritual embodiments adapted to the mental stage of certain epochs, are these truths to remain for ever thus confined and distorted, when the old expressions and assertions have become a patent hindrance? Let us liberate the truth at last, and see how it can make good by its own inherent appealing power.

VIII

THE ARBITRARY AND THE MAGICAL

IT is a remarkable and disconcerting fact that in an age when science has entered more fully into its kingdom than ever before, when education is more widespread, and when indeed in some quarters an excessive rationalism is feared as the most dangerous enemy, at this very time there should be an immense recrudescence of superstition. Does science assume and teach the law of cause and effect? Many prefer magic, which though at a primitive stage it may imply a groping consciousness of causation, is now from any intelligent point of view its virtual denial. Does a rational education aim at a growing power of judgment which can weigh evidence, distinguish true from false, important from trivial, worthy from unworthy? Many prefer subjection to arbitrary authority, a seeing, thinking and feeling according to unexplained orders. Does the very nature of the mind demand an understanding of its experience? To many, it is signs and wonders, mysteries—the more unintelligible the better—that are more interesting; before them they bow and gape, and their intellects sink into abeyance, if not atrophy. Does advancing knowledge or critical examination threaten to discover a reasonable explanation of the phenomenon? Its fascination

THE ARBITRARY AND THE MAGICAL 83

evaporates. It is not the wonders of science that appeal, but the wonders of unreason. A world of tricks, where none can trace the how or why, is preferred to one of ordered purpose, where intelligence can increasingly grasp the wonder of the design and of its execution. Is there any need to emphasize the fact that here you have a tendency as destructive of the true spirit of religion as it is of the claims of reasoned knowledge?

My thesis is that one of the great services that reason should render to the needs of to-day is the combating of this tendency. And this not so much by direct attacks upon or exposures of the absurdity of the more extreme exhibitions of this weakness, as by inducing the more normal and reasonable systems of religious thought and practice to purge themselves of all traces of the same mental attitude. If the greater and more enlightened bodies retain relics of ancient practices and beliefs, which, however some may reinterpret them, make their general appeal as cogent by their very irrationality or operative in the way of magic, how can they protest when others run out into wild excesses? Are the others not following more wholeheartedly in their footsteps? If they themselves are frightened of causal explanations, suspicious of reasoned thinking, assertive constantly of something more reliable than the ordinary mental processes of seeking truth, can they be surprised if these ways of thinking are carried to their natural conclusions? If they are inclined to uphold the arbitrary authority of ancient records or superhuman utterances or august organizations, they must share responsibility for the fact that there is so common a preference for the decisive word of some founder—whether a genuine prophet, a narrow-minded fanatic, or an eloquent and wily charlatan—rather than the humbler and saner methods of gaining the treasures of wisdom and peace. Once commit yourself to the notion of an external authority whose word is to be accepted on grounds, if any, quite other than reason's opinion of its weight, and what is to prevent the multiplication of such authorities? There is no basis for distinction. One man or woman who wields it can put up as good a case as another; indeed the necessity of a case hardly arises. Anyone can claim to be the mouthpiece of God: his or her ability to make others believe the statement is not a guarantee of its truth. And we, the Christian Churches, have laid, or at least strengthened the foundations of the habit of taking religion in spoonfed fashion, doled out by those who know or who are accredited agents, to those whose simple duty it is to receive.

Where are we going wrong? It is obviously not that the claim to be the recipient of revealed truth must be an inadmissible one; nor that those who listen to the prophet or teacher and become his disciples are *ipso facto* open to criticism. The question is how far the authority that is wielded is intrinsic in the very appeal of the message, and how far it is due to irrelevant and extraneous factors, such as the venerableness of an institution or the magnetic nature of a personality, which however valuable in winning an entrance for the message, giving it a testimonial as it were, have no bearing upon its truth. Reason is not concerned to depreciate anything that can communicate vision from one to another, but it must be real vision. Take hold of another's thoughts by all means, as long as we can make them our own: but we can never do that if we will not even consider what is their intrinsic value or whence they derive it.

What is the explanation of this feature found in that very human nature for which we have claimed that reason is its most distinguishing characteristic? The claim may still be valid, even though the capacity is in a very primitive stage, and its exercise hampered by many other natural tendencies. Men have feelings which, besides being an avenue to or an adjunct of the deepest experiences, are also liable to clog or distort the free working of the understanding. They have a certain basic inertia, which may have some value as a steadying influence, but which assuredly induces apathy, self-contentment, a static unadventurous mind. Thus they fear thought and shrink from responsibility. What a comfort to have our minds and souls in another's charge! They have a responsiveness to suggestion, a degree of helplessness in face of arresting and audacious appeals, a subservience to a dominating spirit, a submissiveness to the herd mind—*moutonisme* it has been called; these things may put them at the mercy of those whose influence is along emotional rather than intelligent lines. Such faculties or tendencies may be the servants of good if used with understanding; but not otherwise.

Many, by reason of this inertia or for lack of opportunity to grow, remain at a childish stage where credulity seems almost boundless, and the love of marvels never rises above that of the infantile, or of the adult when in hours of relaxation he has deliberately surrendered to the spirit of magic.

It would not be profitable to attempt an arraignment of our age in this matter of superstition; but of its prevalence there can be no doubt. Impute it to the War if you like, but there ought to have been time to recover our mental balance; or to the increased strain of life, bidding men take short cuts to avert disaster: but will the Churches acquiesce in the maxim that man's extremity is superstition's opportunity? How far this surrender is seriously meant it is difficult to say; sometimes it seems a game: nor is it easy to decide how far the dabbling in the occult arises from a genuine desire to extend the bounds of knowledge, or from a belief that here we may gain touch with the unseen world and so renew our faith.

Take, however, two examples. It is a melancholy thing that a movement which arrogates to itself the name of Christian Science should have owed at any

THE ARBITRARY AND THE MAGICAL 87

rate a large proportion of its popularity, not to any true teaching as to the power of mind over matter which it may contain, but to the imposition of contradictory and unprovable if not meaningless doctrines on the authority of one person—a person whose intelligence was incapable of well-founded and consistent beliefs, but was well adapted to playing upon the weaknesses of the popular mind. Nor is it as though this religious creed proved its rationality by being morally elevating in any comprehensive sense. On the contrary it is seriously defective. Those, as Mr. Fisher says, "who value beauty, compassion, good sense and truth must look in another direction": and again, "health has ousted charity as the main concern."

Thousands in the so-called Christian public are wedded to the idea that Christ is to come again shortly. They have no conceivable reason for thinking so: there is none. Any passages in the New Testament that appear to mean that plainly refer to a then imminent event, and have long ago been falsified. Is there any explanation other than the natural uncriticized love of the marvellous—past, present or to come—coupled with the unconscious desire to shirk the worry of a continued life of steadfast effort and communal responsibility? That may be readily explicable or even pardonable in view of the perplexities and despairs of the time. But it is none the less shirking.

But to come back to the responsibility of the

average Christian organization. Let me take, with no desire to be censorious, but in the belief that these things demand candid treatment, the practice of infant baptism. Let me ask whether the emphasis laid upon this as an essential sacrament of the Church does not produce the result that parents faced with the immediate danger of the death of an infant unbaptized send urgently for a clergyman or minister. Further, whether this does not mean that they believe an external act which cannot by any possibility influence the infant soul to be nevertheless a passport to Heaven. Such a conception would seem inevitable in the case of the full sacerdotal view, and I should imagine that there would be a general probability of it wherever baptism is made a regular institution. But wherever it is found, is it anything else but magic? At the very least it implies the view that the management of the affairs of the universe is hopelessly irrational and arbitrary.

Reverting to the other aspect of the irrational, the power of authority, and the tendency to bow to it without personal conviction, let us not be misled by the analogy of the weight of scientific opinion which we accept without being able to follow the evidence or reasoning which has led to the conclusion in question. There we believe ourselves to have good grounds for the conviction that the scientists have studied the matter thoroughly and arrived at their results by defensible reasoning.

THE ARBITRARY AND THE MAGICAL 89

Moreover we accept their opinion subject to revision at any time in the light of fuller knowledge. The belief rests on inherent grounds of rationality, not on any dictum that "we say so, and you must take it as the truth of God because we say so." If Christian authority will abandon all claim to tame acceptance, all pretensions to be a sole depositary of truth by supernatural arrangement, all assertion of being infallible, the case will be different. No one, who stands for the right of private judgment and individual response, and the supreme value of genuine conviction, wishes to ignore the evidence of other men's experience. The cumulative and sifted experience of the past is not to be thrown aside. But what is essential is that it be used intelligently. Only thus can error be eliminated; only thus can our beliefs have the potency of inner convincement.

It is claimed for the Roman Catholic Church that it is an instrument for the sanctification of its members, partly by "quickening and stimulating the mind to supernatural activity by an outward rule of truth." Instruction and guidance may indeed stimulate and quicken: but that the compelled acceptance of dogmas without permission to question or test them can make the mind more alive is to the present writer beyond belief.

Even with the admission of fallibility, it is still possible to exalt unduly the insight and consequent authority of the few, and the duty of the many to admire, accept and act accordingly. Mankind is divided into the teachers and the taught. Professor A. E. Taylor writes: "Clear-eyed spiritual vision seems to be at least as rare as penetrating mathematical insight or exquisite musical sensibility."[1] It is impossible to accept this. There is variety; there are spiritual geniuses—though it does not follow that their interpretations are valid. But this religious oligarchy will not do. Common moral experience, undeveloped, overlaid, uncomprehended as it may be, is immensely significant even if only for its potentialities; the power of inner response is universal; the humblest and least brilliant has a capacity in the realm of the spirit which is happily free from the limitations of such spheres as mathematics and music. Here we are not tied down for ever to a certain level of ability or attainment. We can at the very least enter in where the genius has opened the door: but we do really get inside. The dependence on real vision and personal conviction is no cheating and disappointing illusion: it is a true opening for everyone.

One additional aspect of the problem in conclusion. It is urged that those types of Christian evangelism which have laid greatest stress upon the non-rational element have been just those which have shown the greatest vitality. Whereas where the daylight of reason has been in the ascendant, faith and activity have faded and died. "By their

[1] *The Faith of a Moralist*, Macmillan & Co.

fruits ye shall know them." In reply to this, I would ask whether the champions of these views are prepared to judge other movements by their popular appeal. What of the six hundred Christian Science healers in Chicago? Some gospels succeed by ministering to healthy needs: others by gratifying unhealthy desires. Let me also repeat what has been said before, that there has been no suggestion that reasoning could take the place of experience; reason does not claim to dispense with the given—it illuminates and uses it; nor is there any desire to belittle the rôle of feeling and the direct appeal to the personal life. If reason neglects phenomena of the spiritual life which are real and vital, it cannot do otherwise than go astray both in the framing of theories and in the ordering of life. But I would suggest that the success of the movements which have been indicated—such as Wesleyanism, Evangelicalism and the Salvation Army—has been due in so far as that success has been true, valuable and lasting, not to any refusal of the rational, but to the fact that they stood for a definite message which contained at least an element that appealed to real inner needs and met them truly, and that they proclaimed this with assurance. What that element was is another matter, but I refuse to believe that it was something incompatible with enlightenment. There is nothing irrational in seeing facts and building upon them. In so far as these revivals depended upon dogmas that will not stand before the progress of rational thought, they have not lasted or will not last; moreover what is false carries evil with it: with the good they have done, bad will have been mingled. Men have no doubt been restrained from sin by fear of the material flames of Hell: but that does not alter the fact that the true motives of morality and religion were being hindered from having due course. As in the operation of Gresham's law, bad reasons have turned out good ones.

No one will dispute the difficulty of the problems involved in this issue of authority and tradition versus personal search and conviction, nor in the kindred question of felt experience versus intelligent interpretation. But if we would take our place on the side of the intrinsic value of truth, we shall not hesitate as to the path to be followed. If we understand the meaning and power of individual conviction, we shall not dream of advocating an unthinking surrender to an authority that overrides and sets at nought the intellect. To set store by experience and to know the worth of a mind that in some measure sees the meaning of that experience,— these are complementary beliefs which we shall cherish. But for the arbitrary and irrational we have no use.

IX

THE UNITY OF THE MIND

THE suggestion has been made that the intellect can render a service to humanity in the working out of a sound psychology, in which the irrational elements of the mind shall fall into their right place as raw material, and reason and conscious purpose shall assume their due supremacy as fashioners of life. Is there something unscientific about this, a suspicion of treachery to the very claims of reason itself? Are we guilty of the proposal that as we take a certain view of what we should like the mind to be, of what it would be a good thing if the mind was, we had better see to it that a psychology is propounded which shall present that case? Of course, you say, the intellect can render a service by providing a true account of the mind, but that will be by impartial investigation and faithful following of the evidence, not by enslavement to preconceived notions: otherwise it is not reason that is at work, it is prejudice.

This is obvious, and may be a warning that should be kept in mind. Nevertheless it is possible that those who are concerned for a science of mental and spiritual phenomena which shall serve the interests of morality and religion, are retaining their hold upon certain supreme values, which others, for whatever reason, are failing to appreciate. It may be—we can hardly deny the possibility—that those who are zealously following out new clues to the meaning and potency of instinct or the unconscious in the making of life and character, are neglecting other elements which do not interest them or which do not fit into the theories they are developing. A behaviourist, for instance, may fail to see that he himself, a theorist seeking to make his ideas appeal to other minds, is a fact which hardly fits into his creed. A psychologist who is impressed with the profound penetration of the sex instinct into every quarter of man's life—all its tendencies and reactions—may be oblivious of the real meaning of human comradeship at its best, when the whole being of one responds to that of another, the affinities of mental and emotional life are at work, thought answers to thought, sympathy to sympathy, character to character, and the animal, whatever its necessary, natural and originating place, is subordinate and incidental. The retention of a high ideal may be an avenue to the true conception of reality.

It is with great hesitation that one approaches a task of this kind, that of indicating the ways in which an intellect bent upon serving the best interests of morality and religion can help towards a sound psychology. And this partly for the reason already named—the risk of standing for a pseudo-science based upon preconceptions, partly because a convincing treatment of the subject would involve an ability to give a detailed criticism of modern theories, to which no claim is made. It may be that some of the comments about to be put forward are applicable not so much to the theories of the originating thinkers, as to popular impressions of these theories, which are guilty of superficial interpretations and hasty deductions. Nevertheless even these latter are of some importance.

There is, for example, the belief that instincts require recurrent satisfaction: if left unstimulated and inactive for long, they are supposed to accumulate a surplus energy which must find an outlet, and the only question is whether the outlet is to be of a lower or higher type. Whatever may be said subsequently about sublimation and an integrated self, to have enunciated this theory, or anything that sounds like it, is to have let loose a very dangerous germ. Is there a mistake somewhere? or have we to make the best of a situation that seems as difficult for the moralist as original sin itself? Surely the theory errs in that it regards all instincts as of a nature identical with certain bodily appetites. An instinct in itself is a mode of unanalysed response of the organism to stimuli of a particular kind. Apart from the coming of the stimuli there is no particular reason why the vital force of the organism should find its way through that channel rather than any other. But what of hunger and sex? The answer is plain. In the case of bodily appetites, the stimulus is within the organism, and is physiologically recurrent; but that does not apply to instincts as such. There is no storehouse of selfishness or fear or curiosity or suggestibility or pugnacity which is continually filled and continually insisting upon emptying itself. In the absence of provocation we do not fill our vials of wrath to the overflowing point. May we not draw the conclusion that it is justifiable, as Mr. Campbell Garnett says, to "assert the possibility and the value of sheer moral restraint by means of turning attention to some other thing and forgetting the temptation?"[1] That is just what restraint very often is, a resolute turning of the eye of the mind and the rudder of the will in a new direction. Apart from questions of bodily appetite, which are partly physiological and will be touched on later, the only restraint to be condemned is that which centres the mind on the temptation when it ought to be diverted, or that which circumscribes the whole activity of the self and leads either to deadness or revolution.

There is both in the theory here criticized and in other quarters a tendency to dwell upon the *vis a tergo*, and to identify that in a given case with a supposed particular instinct that must be satisfied. This may cause us to neglect the problem of the environment which may stimulate or be such as to avoid stimulating; it may mean that we pass

[1] *Instinct and Personality*, George Allen & Unwin.

over that unifying of the mind by a comprehensive aim in which the purpose implicit in the instinct may be brought to light and given its fitting place and in which the central urge of the whole nature may find undiscordant satisfaction. In some of the so-called instincts indeed the stimulus would seem to be mentally internal, or to involve something like a real understanding of the situation. Curiosity is aroused by no one definable type of object; the thirst for knowledge is found at headquarters; the instinct of self-preservation is attached to no specific stimulus nor shows itself in any one type of response. Here we are in the region of what Professor Hocking calls "central instincts" or "necessary interests"; and the more they are examined the clearer it becomes that "they are not distinct and separable entities," but channels of some one fundamental urge which is the very activity of life. The more clearly we see this, the more we shall emphasize the thought that the mind is one, that its growth is a matter of the interpretation of experience in which the conscious factor should play, and does play, an increasing part. "Will," to quote the same author again, "is only the original and permanent purposiveness of the self made definite to the self by its own experience; it is what that purposiveness has always meant, and it begins therefore with experience, and develops with it so long as the individual continues to learn his own mind."[1]

[1] *The Meaning of God in Human Experience,* Yale University Press.

The native activity is engaged in turning into the directed effort.

It can hardly be doubted that the present stress upon the unconscious—as well as that upon the instinctive basis of the mental structure—is fraught with serious possible consequences. To some it has even come as a convenient way of evading responsibility. Men have sought to shirk their personal answerableness in many ways, by blaming now God, now the devil, and now the government. It has been left for our own time to find comfort in that mysterious receptacle of heterogeneous oddments, known as the unconscious. I need hardly say that in these comments I am not so foolish as to be animadverting upon those implications which have resulted in real healing work, or in a new understanding of the importance of early impressions upon the child mind or intense experiences at any stage. Nevertheless this stress has tended to divert men's minds from the thought of the conscious control of life by deliberate purposes and guiding ideals. If there are influences from the unconscious which are playing disturbingly upon the balance of mind or character, it is important that they should be unearthed. In so far as the analyst is assisting this, he is in line with our appeal for the control by conscious purposes. We must look inner facts in the face. No "lies in the soul," no festering sores must be allowed to go unprobed. But let us consider one feature of the line of thought we are criticizing.

It is that the descriptions given of the way in which crude or dubious motives are glossed over by a "rationalizing" process, have tended to belittle or even degrade the place of reason in ordering conduct.

The conspicuous place given to the origins and roots and primitive forms of life's activities and emotions, suggests to many that it is here that you meet the real thing—the rest is illusory and misleading imagining. Find a beginning in mud or animal appetite or strife or childish superstition or parental domination, and there you have the true quality laid bare. Yet the fact remains that it is in the highest developments that the real nature of things is revealed, as important a truth in psychology as in biology, philosophy or any other realm of thought into which growth and evolution enter. Nor is there any reason why the nature of a suggesting motive should be considered as branding the final decision of the will. If the desire to get your name before the public suggests—consciously or unconsciously—that you should make a speech or write to the papers or take a strong line on some public question, that does not necessarily mean that the action taken is to be labelled accordingly. It may be very difficult to know whether you are judging yourself honestly or no. But it is still possible that even with a dubious suggesting motive you have fairly faced the question whether it is right to take this course. It is the genuineness of the governing purpose that is the test, and it must be approved in the forum of the open soul.

It is stated in some quarters that a man tends to condemn failings and sins to which he has himself a strong inclination; that this inclination, checked as to direct expression, finds an outlet in fastening upon evidence of the evil thing in the lives of others. Is this true in the normal cases that most of us have known? Is disapproval of lying an indication of a bent towards deceit? does an expressed hatred of cruelty spring from a sadistic tendency thrust down into the underworld of the mind? are the loose-livers, or those who would be so if they dared, particularly severe upon sexual delinquents? There may be pathological facts which require explanation on these lines. The actual expression of censure may spring from very dubious motives; the tone of the condemnation may derive acidity from an inner discord in the judge's mind. But I am certain that, as loosely stated, there is an element of falsity about this doctrine, and a risk that it may tend to undermine the belief in the genuineness of the moral judgment. The good remains an essential value in life which reason or conscience or the moral sense finds, and on which it bases its pronouncements. Their import and validity and their imperative quality are among the supreme possessions of our complex endowment.

Let us accept all the added light we can find upon the raw material of the mind; but if we take this raw material to be more than it is, if we regard it as in some sense the exclusive real stuff, we are passing over the most significant facts of all. The distinctive feature of the human spirit is its capacity for perpetual self-judgment, so that every experience leaves its trace of satisfaction, or dissatisfaction, and standards are formed and ideals envisaged beyond the attainments of the present. Ideas and ideals are no idle dreams, but potent forces. The organizing of mind and character is a real thing. In the unity of the permanent self is found the uprising master of the situation, and the arbiter of conflict whose award is content or discontent. In conscious purposes, woven together into the texture of character, lies the hope of the future; here is the growing point of life. Not in blind forces acting from behind (though they are there and we must know them for what they are), but in visions of the future drawing men on in the path of progress and the conscious ordering of life under the harmonizing hand of reason, is to be found the significant and fruitful element upon which emphasis should be laid. That the power of the rational is far from what it should be is plain, but this is no ground for deriding it. Rather let us exalt it the more. It is the seed of true manhood. Its duty is not to oust or supersede the vital force of our being that seeks after life and ever more life, but to unify what would otherwise be incoherent and clashing impulses, and to guide these forces into the way wherein man's nature will find itself and therefore its deepest satisfaction. On a deeper view still it is itself perhaps a part of that urge of life which is more than all the stirrings and drivings of the instincts, and which as it ceases to be blind and acquires the gift of sight, values and seeks the good things of the spirit.

> Thy nature-which through fire and flood
> To place or gain finds out its way,
> Hath power to seek the highest good
> And duty's holiest call obey.

X

THE UNSEEN WORLD

RELIGION may be regarded as concerned with our contact with the unseen. But in what sense? There are many other important things that are invisible besides those of what we call the spiritual realm. The laws of mathematics, the theory of evolution, the organic factor in a living creature, the cruelty of a slave-trader, the meaning of Beethoven's Symphonies, the happiness of a child, the character of Nansen, the genius of Einstein,—all these things are beyond the range of the five senses. There may be visible or audible evidence that causes or suggests their presence or their truth, but they themselves are not matters of sensation. When we think about it, indeed, it would appear that the majority of the greatest things in life are unseen, unheard, unmeasured and unweighed. And even where the object stands unmistakably before our eyes, it is our valuation of it which counts, and that appreciation and the worth that it discovers are not matters of sight. If we pressed further with this line of thought, we might be led to discuss and try to establish the interrelation of value and reality; but here the point suggested is a simple one, viz., that the range of the unseen things which are of deep and lasting significance is far wider than merely those we call religious. If then the unseen in the spiritual sense should turn out to be of the same type as these other invisible elements which seem at the very heart of reality, and not some quite distinct kind of entity, is there any ground for surprise or uneasiness? Such a view may at any rate be a beginning, whatever higher conceptions may develop from it.

It was hinted in a previous chapter that at times the spiritual unseen seemed to be imagined as a world of celestial beings which new powers of vision would reveal, and it was urged that one duty of the intellect was to lead to something deeper and truer. These contrasted approaches raise a similar issue to that discussed in the chapter on Ideas or Men, but here with rather a different scope and implication.

We have, in our average unaroused state of intelligence (and some would say we always must and ought to have), an invincible preference for the concrete, and an inability to lay hold of the immaterial and what may seem abstract in character. "While the head demands the universal," it has been said, "the heart yearns for the particular." We like embodiments, events, transactions—things we can see or weigh or date or at least imagine in terms of time and space. We shy at capacities, tendencies, aspirations, spiritual laws and forces, eternal values: they seem little more than words, airy nothings, and at best we think them real in but a shadowy sense. There may be justification for the contention that all reality is in individuals, and that there and there only do these laws and forces and universals exist. Nevertheless it is only in our ability to see the universal in the individual that we shall win any entrance into the truth. The capacity thus to see and grasp universals is essential: knowledge implies it. If so, the preference alluded to is a possible source of weakness and deserves examination. But it is not at bottom a difficulty about abstraction: it is largely a matter of believing in the reality of the things of the mind.

Is a thought a real thing, as real as a brick, more real perhaps? Are ideas of such a nature that they have an influential impact upon human lives? The answer to the question "Do we or do we not regard the Universe as essentially spiritual?" may depend in part on some such simple matter as this: the difficulty may lie here rather than in some metaphysical hesitation. It may be noted in passing that one cause of confusion is the failure to distinguish between a thought as a momentary flash in consciousness, and thought as a mental content with something of the continuity of substance.

This preference for the material and concrete is very plain in the history of religious thought on its lower levels. Prophets and thinkers have frequently called men to deeper truths, but as a rule it is their metaphors which have survived as acceptable, and these have been retained in a crude and literal sense. The golden calf is more popular than the holy of holies. Let us note some examples. Take first such an issue as the origin or explanation of sin and inner discord. The significance of the play of self-consciousness upon natural and un-moral innocence is a difficult conception: Adam and Eve and the serpent are easier. Or again, the thought of the uplifting and perfecting of life. The ideal that beckons us onward and keeps us ever on the move is an intangible thing compared with a picture of a millennium that can almost be dated. Here is the added distinction that the one involves activity and co-operation, the other but a lazy and irresponsible hope. What energy the latter does elicit goes to the appropriate interpretation of the books of Daniel and Revelation, and possibly of the great Pyramid! The inevitable grinding of the mills of God,—the working out of the law of cause and effect in spiritual things,—these are objectified and perverted into a court of justice presided over by the Almighty and the pronouncing of a sentence to everlasting flames or paradise—or some modern attenuated equivalent. Some of the most serious instances of this intellectual inertia are to be found in men's attitude to Jesus. The divineness of his personality has to be clinched (and shorn of its human value) by a miraculous story of his birth. All the stress laid upon such an extraneous and irrelevant ground of worship is subtracted from and interferes with the true reverence for the

THE UNSEEN WORLD

intrinsic qualities of his life and message. The fact that the tragedy of his death was in reality the culmination of his victory and only made his living power more universal and enduring is transformed into (and I suggest obscured by) the stories of the Resurrection. It is true that "I, if I be lifted up" is not generally taken as referring to the Ascension! Yet the triumph of his apparent failure is covered up by the supposed necessity of a miraculous recovery, which nullifies or at least reduces the reality and significance of his death. Nor have all Paul's spiritual interpretations of the risen life sufficed to prevent this. That the sense of tragedy and failure had to be transformed into the conviction of real triumph and abiding power, and that this did in fact happen, is true and immensely significant. But to regard this as coming about by a reversal and annulment of the tragedy, rather than a truer insight into the heart of the matter, is, quite apart from any criticism of the narratives, to spoil its real and revealing message.

To many again the idea of salvation as a continual healing and saving process presents no reality to grasp; at least there is an absence of immediate appeal which leaves the emotions unaroused. Sometimes, however, one may suspect that it is not so much an intellectual difficulty in grasping the idea, as a moral shrinking, such as we have seen in other connections, from the unexciting prospect of continuous effort. "The inevitability of gradualness" does not always commend itself. Instead of this, salvation has to be represented in terms of a celestial transaction and the rescue of an entity called the soul by a single specific event, a simplification of the issue tempered only by the uncertainty of one's own inclusion in the happy band. I would go further and say that our very ideas of the Holy Spirit and of God are limited, if not perverted, by this same tendency. The power of divine influence is not thought of as really at work in the hearts and consciences of men, as the intrinsic appeal of the good, as existing and operating in the very tissue of men's lives, but as an extraneous force that interferes in the way of occasional and uncaused warning, stimulus or enlightenment. The conception of God's personality is so held as to involve an objective separateness. His transcendence is interpreted not as meaning the glorious superiority of an ideal beyond our reach or an inward power far exceeding our used capacities, but as involving a metaphysical detachment. As a consequence worship tends to become an external bowing before superior power and standing, and prayer an appeal to another to do for us what we should do for ourselves.

So too our whole attitude towards the moral life, personal responsibility and the working of cause and effect in character suffers. If anyone proposes to spell "Holy Spirit" without capitals, or to translate the term into the Enthusiasm of Humanity or the spirit of unselfish service, or declares that it has been uttering itself in every moral endeavour since the world began, he is thought to be whittling down a precious doctrine of the Church. That there may be great varieties in the degree to which a man has perceived and submitted himself to this influence of the Highest, and that these variations may be of the deepest importance, is not for a moment denied. The point it is desired to make here is the tendency—and the unhappy tendency—to exclude the divine activity from the continuous stream of the moral life. Let us put the same point another way. Is there some difference between the Spirit of Christ working through the centuries in the hearts of men, and the Mind of Christ which we are exhorted to have in us and which we shall have in so far as we dwell with understanding upon his life and personality and the expanding meaning of his message as its implications have been increasingly understood? Do we think of him as a ghost-like entity making mysterious contacts here and there, or as living in the soul through knowledge, a mental possession, superior only in its profound spiritual effects? Is it in fact useful to remain content with phrases about the Holy Spirit, regardless of the operative factors of the inner life of which not only psychology but the normal consciousness of the thinking mind is well aware, as if in fact the Holy Spirit was something quite apart from them? Is the coming in of God an intrusion, however much He may seem more vividly present at one time than another, in any other sense than that the higher life is always intruding upon the lower? Can we consider the nature and working of the mind on the one hand, and supplement this by occasional contacts with something which intervenes from another sphere, and which is outside the scope of our psychological survey? To do this is according to the view that is here put forward to make a false and unfortunate individualization of the forces at work in the unseen world, and to introduce a disastrous dualism into the unity of the spirit.

Whether or no all these examples meet with acceptance, it should be plain that there is a great task lying before the forces of intellectual education, viz.: to lead men away from beggarly elements to a fresh and deeper grasp of spiritual things, to discover indeed what "spiritual" means. Too often it is taken in a thoroughly departmental sense, whereas its essence is embracement and wholeness and its reference restricted, if at all, only by tone and temper, not by functions or faculty. Thinkers to-day speak much of values, of Beauty, Truth and Goodness. Have our average minds risen to an understanding of what sort of things these are, and that they really exist? I am not suggesting that they exist apart from persons, though if we confine our attention to man, we should have to admit that before man appeared they must have had at least a potentiality of existence—and where that leads we must not here discuss. But I am suggesting that they are real things at work in the spiritual lives of persons. To conceive of love as a real power is indisputably true and incomparably fruitful, even though we know that it must mean the attitude of one personality to another or in a modified sense to some object or absorbing interest.

Professor Whitehead says: "God in the world is the perpetual vision of the road which leads to the deeper realities." There is no need to commit oneself as to the adequacy or otherwise of this statement, but can it be said that common religion is finding language of this kind intelligible? There is surely ground for urging that it ought to move or be moved more and more clearly in that direction: and I am confident that the result would be that many within the present realm of so-called religion would gain a closer contact with reality, and that many deeply spiritual thinkers who are outside would feel free to enter.

The most serious opposition to the suggestions of this chapter will come from those who maintain in Mr. Collingwood's words, "the imaginative nature of religion which inevitably personifies abstractions, or presents ideal distinctions in the guise of concrete objects." This may be admitted as what may be called an educational method. It remains essential that the mind should not be in bondage to its images,—idolatry takes many forms,—but make them the servants of a deeper and more fruitful understanding.

XI

RITES AND SYMBOLS

THE considerations which have been advanced in favour of ideas as against their concrete embodiments, of thinking, in other words, rather than being content with pictorial imagery—though not at all to the exclusion of the latter—lead naturally to the problem of rites and symbols. In them we have a deliberate adoption of a policy which seeks to add continuity and vitality to spiritual experiences by linking them—I use a non-committal phrase—with certain material objects or with regular and presumably impressive outward acts. No one can write in any critical fashion of this practice without being conscious that he may be slurring over the symbols that he values himself, and animadverting upon those with which he has no sympathy. Also he may be forced to recognize that the love of the symbolic is so widespread that it may indicate a need so rooted in human nature that it is foolish and vain to contend against it. How far these possibilities are recognized and met in what follows must be left to the reader to judge. With the first I shall attempt to deal; of the latter it need only be said that it is dangerous to assume that the common practices of men are *ipso facto* to be approved, or that exaggerations of tendency cannot be bad, because the tendency is deeply rooted. Upon that theory few advances would ever have been made in the standards or institutions of humanity. Let me add that there is no thought in this discussion of making a rigid separation of the inward and the outward, the spiritual activity from the external act. The self embraces its environment. Character is action. Value is found by spirit in life and the world. Indeed it is one of the most fundamental objections to the consecrating of special things or deeds that it obscures the discovery of the sacred or the enjoyment of inspiration anywhere and anywhen.

The origins of these rites are various, and need not detain us at length. In so far as they are based on the commands or supposed commands of founders or leaders, they are examples of the influence of sheer authority; and what has been already said under that head has application here. There are indeed few things less in keeping with the method and spirit of Jesus than the laying down of authoritative rules or the establishment of compulsory ceremonies. Let us in any case examine these rites on the not unreasonable assumption that they must prove their value for the world to-day. The pragmatic point of view is surely justifiable in the realm of practice.

This is not in any way to cut ourselves adrift from the past. If it can be shown that established rites are essential for the preservation of the heritage of the past, a safeguard lest the insight of the seers and the stored experience of generations or the memory of significant events be let slip, that will be a strong point in their favour. They will then take their place along with other institutions, the very function of which is so to organize and embody what would otherwise be transient glimpses of good—experiments of which no advantage was taken—that mankind in each age can build anew upon foundations that have stood some test, or the individual have a standing ground or reliable stepping-stones above the flux of occasion and temperament. But all institutions have a dangerous tendency attached to them—that of substituting themselves for their meaning, of outliving their usefulness, or rather of lingering on when virtually dead, of carrying on not by meeting an existent need to satisfaction, or in a way that makes for life and growth, but by the sheer momentum that they have acquired. When this is the case, they become a drag upon the wheels of progress, and their overthrow is not only difficult but probably involves much waste of what was good in the process.

Now the religious rites which we have in mind, and the sacramental or the symbolic element which in some cases at any rate and according to certain views is involved therein, stand in a somewhat different position from other institutions. They are fundamentally concerned not with external acts, which are ordered by social or political necessity for the stability of society or the state, nor even with moral laws and standards which should be so well established in the mind that actions follow almost instinctively. They have to do rather with very intimate and personal matters where freshness, spontaneity and utter sincerity and genuineness at that particular moment are of the essence of the matter. Here, then, it may reasonably be suggested, the dangers of the mechanical and deadening effect produced by a fixed institution are at their maximum. It is of course the old problem of organization and inspiration, but where the whole concern is with the vitalization of the spirit, the case stands upon a special footing.

Is it possible to frame a rule connecting the inward spirit of devotion or dedication with established ritual acts without producing the effect that the outward act comes to be regarded as an intrinsic and necessary part of the spiritual activity, to the detriment of the real purpose intended? The function of the understanding—which is our main theme— is to fasten upon and keep continually in view the real object at which any system is supposed to be aiming, and to test how far this is being successfully compassed.

If the symbolic act is occasional and optional, arising out of particular circumstances or the present sense that here is something that can be made the channel of inward aid, then it is free from the danger that the mechanical may get the upper hand or that the external is intruding upon the spiritual. Spontaneity is retained. The instrument remains an instrument. But if the symbolic act is regarded as a fixture, as essential, that in itself, I suggest, is a proof that the inner meaning is being unconsciously relegated to a secondary—or at any rate only a coordinate—place. In many cases it will be largely or totally obscured. The rite acquires the position of a direct and certain means to spiritual good. Make it regular, compulsory, universal, permanent, and say what you will about its symbolism and of how it is only the spirit behind it that is efficacious, you have nevertheless given it a sacred and exalted place; the symbol has acquired an almost irresistible tendency to oust the spiritual reality and usurp its throne. When, or in so far as, this takes place, you have, as we have already seen, succumbed to the love of magic: and that is unspiritual and irrational. We have spoken in a previous chapter of the rite of baptism. Much might be written of the transmission of power or grace by the laying on of hands. Why cannot the sharers in a Communion Service, who claim to receive inward uplift therefrom, win the same by a united spiritual effort of memory and dedication, without any eating of bread or drinking of wine? Do the material things themselves bring spiritual help? Do they make the mental effort easier? and should it be made easier?

It may be asked at this point whether upon this

view all established and regular practices are to be condemned. They are all liable to become forms out of which the life has departed or which are regarded as of value irrespective of any inner purpose or significance. No doubt there is this serious danger, and it may be difficult to draw an exact line between forms that are necessary and helpful, and rites that have an anti-spiritual tendency. But there is a certain plain distinction. You have on the one side those regular practices which are merely opportunities when the real thing can occur or be presented; and on the other, stress upon the presentation of something which has no intrinsic connection, at best is an external feature with only an outward association, with the ultimate purpose. Even to fix a time for a course of lectures is, I suppose, to bring rigidity into what might have been left fluid; but this is not likely to erect the form into a substitute for the reality. The silence of a Friends' Meeting, while it may at times have been wrongly revered almost as if it were something good in itself, is clearly an opportunity waiting to be used. That is what it consists of: its actual content is what the mind is doing. No doubt it is a form to go to a place of worship, including a Friends' Meeting House, in the sense that it introduces an element of habitual regularized practice into life. But I am not pleading for an abolition of that regularity that steadies life, provides it with a skeleton, and prevents it from being at the mercy of whims and moods and casual desires. To be anxious to make institutions the servants of spontaneity, and not its assassins, to preserve spiritual meanings from being choked by the dominance of outward symbolisms, this is not to be an anarchist, oblivious of the value of habit and accepted order.

I believe that the suggested distinction between those things which are primarily and obviously openings for the activities of the spirit, and those which put what is inherently an alien and irrelevant element into the forefront, is an important one, even though at times the precise line of demarcation may be hard to draw.

George Tyrrell, speaking in 1899 of the abuse of external means of grace, says: "We clutch eagerly at a miraculous medal, a girdle, an infallible prayer, a scapular, a novena, a pledge, a vow—all helps, in their way, all excellent if used rightly as stimulants to greater exertion, greater vigilance, greater prayerfulness; but if adopted as substitutes for labour, for the eternally necessary and indispensable means, then no longer helps, but most hurtful superstitions. Do they stimulate or do they relax our efforts?— that is the one test as to whether we are using such things to our help or abusing them to our hurt. We shall not be saved by anything we hang round our necks, except so far as the grace it conveys to us in virtue of the Church's blessing stimulates us to that exertion and watchfulness by which alone, under God, we are to sanctify and save ourselves."[1]

While recognizing the spiritual position here presented, which will have nothing to do with rites or symbols as substitutes for their meaning and message, one is obliged to ask whether to expect stimulus and help to come through or in necessary association with some detached and accidental thing like a medal or a girdle, or grace and blessing to be conveyed through them by the Church—whether this is not to introduce just that element which the rational thinker must stigmatize as unhelpful superstition, and which is bound to be hostile to a truly inward and spiritual attitude. The symbol regarded as essential, or as capable in itself of being the bearer of inspiration or comfort, insists upon becoming a substitute.

It is often urged that as many good people find help, in the way either of stimulus or of consolation, from the celebration of certain symbolic rites and sacraments, it must therefore be taken as proved that these are sound and justifiable practices. It is impossible to accept this. It has been suggested above that the help really comes from quite other causes, which would operate more freely and with more invigorating effect in the absence of the symbol. For anything we know, the prayer wheels of Tibet may be regarded as a real help by those whose minds are capable of using them as means to a good end. The influence of a particular method

[1] *External Religion; its Use and Abuse*, Sands & Co.

is not to be tested by the example of those who are capable of rising above the defects of any conceivable method, but by the interpretation given to it by the generality of men, and its effect upon their mental outlook. Nor is it admissible that even the former few would not profit by discarding the outward mechanism.

There is one fundamental consideration which has not yet been raised, and which may affect the validity of the views put forward. Is there any reason why the right method for one person should be the right method for another? Why not each according to his need and nature? There is no question, you say, of contradictory opinion. In the sphere of facts and theories we must accept one and reject its opposite. The man who holds that Moses wrote Deuteronomy, and the man who holds that he didn't, cannot both be right. There cannot both be and not be a Hell for unbaptized infants. But is it not possible that for some the method of relying on outward symbolic rites is the best one, while for others it is most helpful to dispense with them? Why not accept these variations tolerantly? This is a point of view that deserves all respect, and no one will wish to dismiss in any particular case the possibility that this may be the right attitude. Nevertheless I believe that there are general truths even on questions of method in spiritual edification. Has not Education some recognized laws of action? Has not practice its principles as much as theory?

Mental activity is better than submissive unintelligent acceptance. A sense of the reality of the inward is not easy to gain and keep, and it will not be encouraged by stressing the essentialness of the outward. It is easy to be satisfied with metaphors and symbols and never to trouble about their meaning. The easy is not necessarily the best. Part of the mind enjoys the effort which keeps it on the stretch: part hankers after the line of least resistance. Which part is to be fostered? He who depends on outward aids may be like one who finds a crutch or a bath chair convenient to his needs and never gains the strength that would come if he tried to walk alone. To say that the strength can only be gained or the will invigorated through these outward aids is to perpetuate irresponsible dependence and therefore to stabilize weakness. Once more let it be urged that, as a matter of fact, where spiritual help is gained, it has probably little connection with, say, the partaking of the consecrated elements: it is the gathered opportunity for a specific effort of commemoration and dedication that has the uplifting influence. Why weaken the real cause by emphasizing the unreal?

All the language of religion, all the approaches to the deep things of the spirit, are and perhaps always must be filled with imagery and symbolism. This may be one of the great gateways by which the truth can enter the inmost places of the soul. But it has its dangers; and my position is that when an act which is only relevant in its symbolism and not in itself, and which is yet concerned with the very spontaneities of the spirit, is made a universal practice, a *sine qua non*, the danger is so accentuated that we had better discard that mode of spiritual treatment, and concentrate definitely and boldly on the inward experience and the meaning that it carries with it. Is this difficult? That many prefer the easier path is no defence. Man has possibilities of effort and of intelligence. Emphasize the understanding side of man's nature, educate it by trusting it more fully, and it will rise to heights otherwise impossible. Let us put away childish things.

XII

A RATIONAL MORALITY

THE fourth service which was suggested for the intellect was the rehabilitation of morality upon a rational basis. The sense of this need is clearly expressed by philosophers and by certain of the more popular educators of public opinion; but it percolates slowly and the official attitude of the Churches still smacks of the old absolutism. Moral and religious conceptions or symbolic representations which served with acceptance in an age when most men were the more or less helpless subjects of autocratic rulers, are singularly out of place to-day. Even the prevalence of dictatorships does not affect the truth of this statement. We have suffered long enough from the idea that morality is an arbitrary and inconvenient system of restraints imposed upon us from without, with the implication which tends, consciously or unconsciously, to accompany this doctrine, that evasion wherever possible is natural if not justifiable. It is a strange thing, for example, that the story of Adam and Eve is seldom if ever judged from this ethical point of view. It is indeed often maintained that, however science or history may assail the literal truth of the narrative, it still remains of value from the spiritual point of view in relation to the coming of sin into the world.

Yet the most serious objection to it, not as an interesting record of a stage in man's moral and religious growth, but as an instrument of education in the twentieth century, is that it makes the commandment of God an utterly arbitrary and irrational prohibition. Once let this idea sink into the mind, particularly the plastic mind of the child, and it will be difficult to eradicate it.

Over against this let us set the thought that the moral law is the stored result of world experience which puts into our hands the clue to human good. This exists not for the subjection of the mind, but for its guidance. This is its inheritance, and is meant for judgment, use and modification. The need of this rational view, so very inadequately grasped as yet, is forced upon us not only by the general tendency to reject ancient inhibitions and indeed the whole conception of moral authority, but by the coming into prominence of a number of new ethical problems for whose solution there is no established formula that carries with it sacred associations or intuitive authority. The practice of gambling is an example of this. While some men condemn it, others ask wherein its evil lies; they will not agree that it is wrong without a clear understanding of the ground for such condemnation. Men who do condemn it are at a loss to defend their position against their fellows. But note the fact that this difficulty does not arise from any features peculiar to this case. What about moral judgments which are of long standing, whose validity is unchallenged? If a man were bidden to supply a convincing reason why lying is wrong, he would probably find it equally hard to give a satisfactory answer. But he will not be so challenged. The intuition against lying stands, and few question it: the condemnation of gambling, if sound, has still to make good its position.

This necessity is spreading. Moral scepticism grows and old personal and social issues assume new shapes. There is a readiness to make moral experiments. "Safety first" gives way to the spirit of adventure and exploration. The divine right of book or person or code, however hallowed by the sanctity of ages, or guaranteed by a character worthy of all reverence, is no longer accepted. Reason is at work. It is true and worth noting that it is at times complicated by an utterly unreflective spirit of revolt, and even it may be an unconscious will to licence. Nevertheless it is at work. "Everything," says Mr. Galsworthy, "being now relative, there is no longer absolute dependence to be placed in God, Free Trade, Marriage, Consols, Coal or Caste." Such a situation may easily become perilous—far more so than the overthrow of many creeds—unless met by a worthy intellectual effort, not merely by a few thinkers or a handful of exceptional teachers, but by all the great organizations which set out to instruct the nation—an effort to lay hold of the intrinsic meaning and value of the good, and to grasp with understanding and make clear to others the individual and social justification of the moral law. I am not of course asserting—let me guard myself once more against such an impression—that the intellect provides a complete recipe for the production of good men and women: but the part that it can play is our subject, and the moral value of an understanding mind has hardly yet been tested. "The function of the moralist," says Mr. Lippmann, "is not to exhort men to be good, but to elucidate what the good is." We need not perhaps set the one against the other, but may join in pleading the practical value of the latter.

It is sometimes imagined that the application of reasoned thought to morality will undermine the sense of responsibility. Once begin to regard human conduct as a sphere where the laws of cause and effect are as surely operative as elsewhere, and how does choice come in? In what sense are we answerable for our decisions? I am not going to enter here upon any real discussion of the problem of the Freedom of the Will; but one or two things may be said. This alleged result can only be supposed to follow by one who conceives the operative causes as external, playing upon a self that is their victim. But they are not; they are in the self, they are the self; they are the organism in action as a conscious entity. Being conscious, it is not in the grip of mechanical compulsion, but why anyone should desire that an act of choice should be proved to be motiveless, appearing out of a blue sky, unconnected with any mental state that had gone before, it is difficult to imagine. Remove the connecting strands which bind together motive and action and consequence, which link past to present and present to future, and responsibility would indeed become meaningless. It is because the act of volition springs from the united elements of the self and is the outcome and expression of character, that we impute responsibility. It is because we believe in cause and effect in the spiritual sphere—however possible it may be to distinguish their mode of operation here from that in outward nature—that we praise and blame, train and instruct, trust or distrust. There is no more merit in the arbitrary in the sphere of moral conduct than anywhere else.

In practice a useful and even necessary distinction may be drawn between self and others. To trace an act to its explanatory antecedents is in our handling or appraising of other people a thoroughly sound proceeding. The readiness to do so will revolutionize—is doing so to some extent—our whole conception of criminal justice and penal treatment. But in making our own decisions, we have nothing to do with causes; we are only concerned with ends to be compassed, methods to be adopted, and the rightness or wrongness of these ends and methods.

Before entering upon any specific moral problems to which this rational treatment should be applied, it may be right to consider a fundamental question as to the very existence of moral principles. To some minds the variations of the moral judgment amongst different individuals, races and ages are so great that they can find no common element. They are thus drawn—or shall we say allow themselves to be driven?—to the conclusion that there is no such thing as one moral standard or basis of judgment. There is nothing but idiosyncracies of taste or custom, between which there is no means of deciding. Or, if they approach the matter from another angle, it may be said that the varieties of human nature and its circumstances are infinite; no two cases are alike; it is impossible to lay down any universal moral laws—there can be none.

To the latter argument, the reply is surely to admit it as a useful warning against the elaboration of absolute rules, to seek rather for central broad principles or guiding and inspiring ideals; but to assert emphatically that there do exist common fundamental qualities of human nature and general similarities of circumstance and personal relationship which make it possible to lay down the conditions essential for the good life of individuals and communities. If it were not so, it is hard to see how life and particularly associated life could be carried on. It postulates something dependable, and its freedom can only live on a basis of order.

As to variations in the moral judgment, are they any more difficult to reconcile with an objective

A RATIONAL MORALITY

standard than the changes and differences of opinion among scientists as to external nature? Because Sir Arthur Eddington differs from Ptolemy, Kepler and Newton and possibly from Sir James Jeans, we do not conclude that the heavenly bodies are a myth. "We may admit," as Hastings Rashdall says, "the validity of the principles of reasoning and of the axioms of mathematics, although many men reason badly, and some cannot even count."[1] In all the heterogeneous approvals and disapprovals that morality has expressed, we see the human spirit recognizing that there is a supreme value, the good, after which it must strive. The distinction of right and wrong, drawn and applied by the practical reason, runs like a constant thread through the whole record of man's thought and action. The significance of his approval of humanity and his condemnation of cruelty, as Lecky has pointed out, is not affected by the shifting nature of what is adjudged humane or cruel. Moral knowledge has to grow just as physical knowledge must. Primitive crudities and present-day controversies no more invalidate the one than the other. That the reality towards which that knowledge approximates is there in some sense, and that man is made to seek it and enjoy increasing dominion over it—these remain truths which the normal mind will scarcely desire to dispute.

Our main concern is that we may confront in a

[1] *Theory of Good and Evil*, Oxford Press.

I

rational manner the specific moral problems which demand solution to-day. No indiscriminate or perpetual questioning is being extolled. A moral intuition is not to be lightly dismissed. That we cannot at the moment connect it with any rational valuation does not stamp it as a traditional prejudice or an irrational emotion: it may be deeply rooted in the nature and experience of men. What is important is our broad conception of morality and our readiness to solve problems, when they arise, in the light of truth. If anyone is disposed to urge that morality is a matter not of reason but of feeling, we must once more distinguish between the two senses of feeling: do you mean an unanalysed intuition, or an emotional element? If the latter, I would assert emphatically that morality is not in essence an affair of feeling but is a judgment of value. If the former, it is true that the moral sense will and should act with habitual and instinctive promptitude, but its utterances are particular judgments in the application of general principles, and the application and the principle must be defensible at the bar of the supreme value.

This leads us naturally to a still deeper and wider discussion of the need of the moment. There is much to be said for a far more widespread study of ethics than obtains at present. What are the advantages which may be derived from it? Is there a direct and practical gain, or is it all mere philosophic curiosity? Though indeed science and religion

A RATIONAL MORALITY

and every phase of conduct and thought seem to be driving us more and more to the conviction that we cannot do without a thought-out philosophy; and what philosophy can be more profitable or necessary than that which deals with the right and the good? I would maintain that to find a first principle of living—if that should be possible—of which all others are corollaries, an ultimate good wherein the rest find their justification, would be a reinforcement of the whole spiritual life. A deeper insight means a stronger grip upon the essential elements of good. An all-embracing aim, well grasped and understood, means that all subordinate aims are fortified, as well as purified, by becoming members of an organic system. The principle of honesty seen and revered in all its fulness not only brings new light into dark places, but bears with it an added strength even in the plainest issues. Departmental morality involves weakness even in the department itself.

It is not suggested that universal principles will be constantly before the mind. They are not going to be habitual motives. They are to govern unseen as a rule; they are implicit in the decisions of the will or in the derivative laws of action. They will not usurp the place that will always remain for deep feeling and determined enthusiasm for definite causes in the service of humanity or the Kingdom of God. But they may bring vision, harmony and power. Someone may raise the query, is there any need to study ethics to find this ultimate principle? Why go to Plato or Butler or Bentham or Bradley? Is not our aim to glorify God? to do the will of God? to follow Jesus Christ? This is not the place to discuss all that is involved in finding satisfaction in these modes of expression. We have already urged that Jesus taught things because they were true; they are not true because he taught them. If he revealed truth, it is for us to understand it as such. Nor do the clashing desires of life come to us as labelled as the will or not the will of God. We need all the means of discrimination and judgment that the mind can furnish; we have powers of reason that are meant to be used in placing particular cases in their universal setting. If "the will of God" is not a mere phrase to cover a traditional virtue, it stands for some supreme standard that presumably is worth an effort to understand in respect of its origin, its implications and its sanctions.

Is not one of the problems which the Christian Churches are called upon to solve to-day—a problem perhaps of method and emphasis rather than of considered doctrine—that of combining full recognition of and reverence for the inspiring power and profound spiritual insight of Jesus, and all that that has meant and will mean to the race and to individuals, with an understanding that the laws of life, whoever discovered them and whoever lays them compellingly upon men's hearts, do themselves stand as it were upon their own feet. Their truth lies in no man's authority, but in the nature of reality. Once grasp this, and these laws acquire a new and rational validity, and reality itself a new meaning and character.

XIII

SOME ETHICAL PROBLEMS

ONE example only has as yet been named in illustration of this need for a rationally grounded morality, viz. the practice of gambling. But in another connection we have touched upon the right attitude to be adopted towards the instinct of sex. Let us take up the tale again, for this is a matter which demands more perhaps than any other the application of such reflection as bases itself upon the values which reason finds, and follows such methods as reason approves. There is no more fundamental issue than this: the institution of marriage and the home is more closely bound up with the needs of man and the healthiness of society than any that can be named. The quality of the inner life, the very tone of the soul, the existence of relationships which elicit the best in human nature, the upbringing of children in an atmosphere of affection, the value of permanence in life—all these things are at stake. This is not said with any idea of prejudging the issue, unless it is prejudice to take the matter seriously. No one will pretend that the inquiry in this case is an easy one. It is not a voyage where reason will find plain sailing. The argument may encounter some threatening waves; rational practice will certainly do so.

Sex is the most compelling and absorbing of human instincts; there is no other so capable of sweeping the whole mind along with it, pouring its emotion into every channel, and drowning every voice of questioning or protest. If this tremendous fact is supplemented by a theory that here you have something of the essential urge of life, it acquires a sort of theoretic sanction for its free exercise and becomes an even more formidable factor for reason to take account of. It seems indeed to challenge the claim of reason to be supreme at all. But we have already denied the right of any instinct to assert itself as a necessary avenue for vital power. There is no element of the mind that can be allowed the last word. That belongs to the whole; only so can anarchy and enslavement be escaped, and order, freedom and growth be ensured.

If there is any impelling instinct which speaks for the whole, it is the will for life, or as Professor Hocking prefers to express it, with careful interpretation, "the will to power." Here is the power, but the guidance lies with reason. The will to life does not of itself know the path to life. To reason is given the task of direction and organization in the service of that good which she, reason, has found in experience, and whose conditions she may progressively work out.

Whatever difficulties there may be in any attempt to solve the sex question on rational lines—and it may of course be urged that only a clear intuition or a powerful counter-emotion can do it in daily practice—one thing is certain, and it must be repeated once more, that neither this nor any other moral perplexity can be settled by quotations from Scripture, pronouncements of the Church or even the unconsidered dictates of some intuitive moral sense which seems authoritative to those who possess it. These things may be good evidence or suggestive signposts, and it would be folly to rule out the lessons of the past, underestimate our debt to the insight of genius or simple devotion, or neglect the pronouncements of the normal conscience. But reason playing upon experience must come to the rescue, as it has always been implicitly seeking to do through the darkness and the twilight of human ethics. "Get wisdom, and with all thy getting, get understanding."

To return to our problem. Here is a case consisting like all other moral issues partly of self-management, partly of relations with our fellows, though indeed it is impossible to separate these elements; one might almost say that the self is our relations with our fellows. The good life which reason and its ideals set before us implies that purposes which integrate have supremacy over instincts which divide. It is the spiritual which gives continuity, meaning, value to life. We know well how physical desire, given the rein and made an end in itself, can shatter the unity of the mind and character, and incapacitate for better things. The good and rational life sets up the personalities of all men and women as having inherent value, as being sacred: and the attitude of mind that expresses this towards our fellows is one of understanding, reverence, selflessness, love. These are the qualities that make for life; they are the fruits of the spirit; they are the friends of reason.

The value of an institution lies in its power to embody and give permanence to truths like these, truths that, though fundamental to the true life, can so easily be obscured in the shortsightedness of the momentary mood or the utter blindness of passion.

It is perhaps rather aside from our main theme, but the familiar truth may be recalled at this point, that the chamber of the soul needs to be not only swept and garnished, but also well furnished and inhabited, lest wandering devils make an entrance. The intellect's share in this work, alike positive and preventive, is obvious, and nowhere more pertinent than in regard to the very present fact of sex.

If the attempt has been mistakenly made to meet the force of this instinct by pushing it out of sight, instead of frankly recognizing its natural place, a still greater danger confronts us in the stress laid by novelists and others to-day on the physical side of love. The older and greater writers were more closely in accord both with ideals and facts; they knew that the best and indeed normal attraction between men and women is that which unites them in the realm of disposition, character, thought, purpose, and the whole direction of life. The more these dominate the situation—even though it be unconsciously and implicitly in one all-compelling set of the mind and heart—the better is the combined meaning of body and soul realized. The physical then falls into its right and natural place as incidental.

Critics who revile, say, the Victorian Age for a furtive, repressed and therefore debased view of sex, often fail to see that our forefathers' attitude at its best arose not from a low but a high conception of this relationship. Reticence may surely spring not from shame, but from reverence for a sacred intimacy that is not to be discussed upon the housetops.

There are grave possibilities of peril even in sex instruction, unless it is so wisely administered as never to outrun its appropriate stage. If a physical act has its right and beautiful place as the intimate expression of a uniting love, we should beware of isolating it: how can its true nature be made a matter of knowledge, except for those to whom that love has come? If it is an accompaniment, how can it be rightly understood and placed, apart from that which it accompanies and which should itself be dominant in thought? To drag the physical perpetually or even prematurely into the limelight is to pervert both it and everything else. That in it may be the ground and origin of love and marriage is irrelevant: we are not concerned with origins, but with meanings, purposes and values for developed life.

The danger of some modern teaching in regard to the repression of instincts—or it may be a misreading of that teaching—is especially serious here. Dr. Douglas White has written some fundamental truths on this point. "On the psychological side, it seems that more neurosis arises from the unethical giving way to the sex drive than from resisting it. You cannot solve the problem by cutting out ethics." He quotes an opponent as saying that all he asserts is that continence demands a heavy price. "He is right, it does. That was recognized by Hesiod long ago: 'Before virtue the immortal gods have placed sweat.' It may demand a severe mental strain; that strain may in some degree react on the general bodily health, though there is no evidence that it produces sexual atrophy or impotence. But is nothing to be gained from the struggle? Surely there is. I do not value abstinence as a thing in itself: I do value it as a preliminary to obtaining in the end the prize of an all-embracing love, physical and spiritual, by which one man can give himself whole and entire to one woman who, on her part, does the same."[1]

There is much else that could be said upon the sanctity and permanence of the marriage tie, the

[1] *Is Sexual Abstinence Harmful?* Association for Moral and Social Hygiene.

central significance of the home, and the needs of the children. But this much has been put forward to illustrate the kind of rational consideration that must be brought to bear on such problems of character, conduct and human institutions. On these lines alone, and not by the clash of arbitrary injunctions and rebellious appetites, is to be found the ground of hope for their progressive solution. If the officials of the Churches had devoted as much energy as they have given to the restriction and refusal of divorce, to proclaiming the profound and saving worth of a reverent and understanding comradeship of love, they would have contributed more to the redemption of individuals and the community. It is in such intimacies of life that its possibilities are either missed or realized.

Another group of urgent questions may just be mentioned, that which concerns our attitude towards offenders. What of prison and the gallows? What of war and international coercion? Or of forgiveness until seventy times seven? There is a considerable readiness to-day to discuss penal methods in the light of reason and experience. The same is true, though less true, of war; but here what is holding up the advance of thought is an unreadiness to seek the real deeps of the argument or to hold to the uttermost to certain principles and values to which men pay homage in private life. I do not say that the increasing sway of reason is the only requisite here: but even the intellectual virtue of consistency would carry the man who is by nature and in ordinary affairs a kindly and self-controlled being a long way on the road to the refusal of war.

But when we reach the claim that we should cherish a forgiving spirit, the old tendency is stronger. Men are still inclined to regard this as a mysterious demand for some impracticable ideal, which there is good ground for postponing to a more convenient season—presumably some distant period when there will be no injuries or enemies to forgive. Yet the real justification of forgiveness is plain, in its release of the forces of good, alike in him who gives and him who receives.

Take again the problem of self-sacrifice. According to the author of the Fourth Gospel, as translated by Dr. Moffatt, Jesus said, "He who loves his life loses it, and he who cares not for his life in this world will preserve it for eternal life." Putting aside as here irrelevant the question of immortality, we may take this saying as emphasizing that he who would really live must not attach undue importance to his own continued existence, must escape from absorption in self into a wider universe. Whether Jesus used these precise words or no, he certainly lived them: and in spite of his untimely and cruel death, everyone would admit that he lived a very real life which was no failure and which counts eternally, in a way that no life of self-centred pleasure seeking or cautious security has done or ever could do.

This thought which may provisionally be labelled

sacrifice, is clearly a central one in the Christian conception. The real obstacle to its acceptance—like many of our most serious perplexities to-day—is an ethical one. A world enjoying emancipation from the restraints—bondage if you like—of many old traditions and conventions, values freedom, thinks of bonds as spoilers of life, wants to make the most of its time here, sets up positive happiness against negative discipline, means to realize itself to the full. What has a gospel of self-sacrifice to say to this? What does such a world want with self-denial? Why forgo things which you might enjoy? Why impoverish life when it might be rich?

In the first place, it is worth while to remind ourselves that all developed life means renunciation in the sense that to succeed in any line we must give up certain possibilities, that we must select and concentrate. So no theory of the right to realize some desire or follow some natural impulse can escape from this necessary opposition. We want to lie in bed, but also to be punctual at our work or to respect the household convenience. We should like more expensive clothes, but also an increase in our library or more savings for an early marriage. Something has got to go. They are all parts of the self, and the ideal of self-expression carries us nowhere until we have decided which self is to be expressed.

The problem, therefore, is not whether we are to sacrifice something—that is inevitable; but rather what we are to sacrifice. The choice is the great thing—what we value most, and what is a lesser good that must be relinquished or an obstacle or discordant element that must be eliminated. Some supreme principle or value which will put each subordinate end in its right place is what we need and must have. To follow this, to gain the best, to achieve the end which we have put first on the list, labour, discipline, hardship may be necessary; ease, pleasure, some amenities of life must be sacrificed.

In the choice of the ideal, we may think of the need of an ordered and harmonious self as better than a discordant multitude of desires and impulses, in which now one and now another gains the upper hand. Or again—and this is even more necessary and fruitful—we may realize that the self is not an isolated being, but a social entity. It is essentially a network of relations. We are husbands, fathers, sons, workers, customers, investors, teachers, pupils, neighbours, citizens, human beings. And the ideal to which we pin our faith has to help us to function well in these various capacities. For the fulfilment of these, for the realization that is of our true selves, we are called upon by the very nature of things to be ready to pay a price—a price of self-control, concentrated effort, the suffering it may be that springs from broadened sympathies, more sensitive feelings, unremitting devotion, readiness to face unpopularity and obloquy.

It seems clear then that self-sacrifice is not an end in itself. There is no inherent advantage in stinting and stunting. To give up is demanded of us, where it is giving up a minor good for a major good, a narrow good for a wider one, a transient good for an enduring one. Our ability to pay the price is the test of the value we set upon the greater purpose. And as a test of our devotion, it bears with it the power to appeal to others in proof of the reality of our professions. It sets the seal upon our message. So in demanding sacrifice of ourselves and recognizing that this carries with it its own appeal and guarantee, we find that there is something in human nature that responds. The call to endure hardness as good soldiers of some great cause is not repellent; it is attractive. We have the capacity for heroism, a readiness, at any rate, to follow heroic leaders, even in a forlorn hope.

Some educational problems which raise a similar moral issue will be touched on in the next chapter. But there is one other burning question of the day that may be mentioned, viz. the right use of Sunday. Apart from the legal and political controversy, is not the real issue whether men need, and can be convinced by experience or persuasion that they need, a time when they can withdraw from the absorbing details of business and even of recreation, consider the meaning of things, and nourish that inward and basic life of the spirit which is deeper than the superficial happenings in time, and

SOME ETHICAL PROBLEMS

broader than the confinements of the little self. Reason with its interest in the profound, the universal and the permanent, should surely have its say.

We should guard against giving the impression that any universal and absolute solutions are to be expected or desired from this rational approach, to take the place of the old arbitrary commandments. Elasticity is inevitable. Experiments, if sincere and serious, are to be commended. A new tolerance, difficult, it may be, to maintain, will be required. Life is movement and always will be; no static Utopia or Heaven is either attractive or possible. But we shall move forwards more quickly and more reliably by the conscious and unhampered exercise of that quality of the human mind which makes for the harmonizing of claims and activities, and creates and re-creates an ideal accordingly. It should be added that it will probably always be necessary for morality to forbid some acts, even though in certain instances they seem harmless, on the ground that they will encourage imitation in cases where the results may be bad.

Does it seem to anyone that this line of thought will tend to reduce the august certainties of the moral law, which filled the soul of Immanuel Kant with awe, to the precarious position of private and momentary argumentation? Does this plea for human reason seem to detract from the high conception of an essentially divine element in human nature which recognizes, responds and reaches out to the good? Or again, are we exalting intellect at the expense of will and feeling? I plead guilty to none of these things. The fact that men have evolved or progressively discovered a moral law with its sense of indefeasible obligation, the fact that principles and ideals have come into being and carry with them a regulative authority and a purifying and exalting power—these things remain, and it is they, and not some detached and alien fact, which are the demonstration of man's higher nature. That they may come to rest upon understanding will but make their value plainer, their claim upon us more effective, and their permanence more secure. Nor has the argument in any way affected their intuitive method of action. I am not asking for perpetual inward discussion. The motives of conduct will seek their own ends. The standards of action will operate directly. The enlightened conscience will speak without hesitation or delay. To accept consciously will surely be to obey the more promptly and unhesitatingly. We shall follow good because we love it for its own sake; but we shall love it more when we know it through and through; and when we question we must know where to look for an answer. A few convictions well grasped and held are worth more than a multitude of unverified creeds or arbitrary commandments.

XIV

WHAT THEN OF EDUCATION?

The more one takes an inward experiential view of religion and of reason as its interpreter, and a modern view of education (though much of it will be found in Plato), the closer does their relationship appear. We might almost adapt a well-known saying and assert that education and religion are one, or neither is anything. Both seek to make the most and best of the human mind and soul. Each fastens upon the value of the individual and the latent possibilities in his nature. Each stresses the need of personal activity as a way to good and an outcome and expression of good. Each is concerned with knowledge, feeling and will, and with their balance and unity in a growing life. The divine in man is not necessarily interpreted as an isolated faculty intervening on occasion, but as the demand of the whole man for the development of all that he has it in him to be. The call of both—education and religion—is to the full functioning of the capacities of body and soul, as uttered by the personal ideal and the laws of that associated life in which personality finds the guidance to its true realization. Each professes to stand for the way of advancement in life, and whether education is a part of religion, or religion a part—or a consummation—of education is almost a matter of words.

The recognized aim of education—as at once inward and comprehensive—goes to establish this intimacy. No serious thinker will regard it as a matter merely of technical preparation or mental agility, or still less of the storing of massed facts. Character must dominate, but to say this is not to relegate to any inferior place the claims of wide and exact knowledge, or of a trained capacity of hand and eye and brain. Character is an all-round affair; so is reason; so is religion. The more their mutual involvement is understood, the better.

Our survey of ethical perplexities leads us naturally to some of the riddles which occupy the attention of educational thinkers and practitioners to-day. The present age is notably concerned with the contrary claims of discipline and obedience on the one hand, and freedom and self-direction on the other. Our point is that this is another moral issue (and here perhaps no one will dispute it—the Ten Commandments are not clear on the point!) to add to those already adduced as examples of the need of rational consideration. It is a fundamental matter for the educator and for all who are engaged in the management of men—statesmen, rulers of dependencies, dictators, governors of prisons, captains of industry, bishops of the Church, fathers of families. We are as a matter of fact in contact here not so much with a new and separate ethical controversy, as with the practical application in human relationships of the principle we have been advancing throughout, that understanding is better than tame acceptance or submission. This practical application carries us into two spheres, separable in thought, although as usual blended in fact: one the direct control of conduct, the other the transmission of thought and knowledge. In each you have the rival doctrines of authority and freedom. In the first sphere, that of the management (if that word does not beg the question) of boys and girls, men and women, the service of the intellect will be to keep in view the value of personality, to study human nature so as to understand wherein the essential elements of value consist, and to work out, by hypothesis and experiment, the best methods of developing that personality. For the rulers of men, the primary duty, as things are at present, is to lay hold as never before of the belief in the worth of every individual man, and cease to be obsessed with mechanisms and abstractions, or dominated by territorial or mass conceptions.

Our task here is more clearly concerned with the presentation of truth. There is a strong case for giving the Humanities a fuller opportunity and a more serious treatment in our schools. The more you do this, the more there comes in the factor of personal opinion. That you are here entering the sphere of moral and personal valuation is the very reason why you lay stress upon this side of education. It is concerned with judgments and purposes, the unravelling of human motive, the estimation of effort and achievement. How can the teacher's own attitude fail to enter in? On the other hand, how far is it his duty, or even permissible for him, to inculcate his own conceptions? Assuming for the moment that he is one who broadly accepts the moral and religious ideas of his own or his father's generation, are we to regard him—is he to regard himself—as the channel by which the tested knowledge and experience of the past is to be passed on to the young? If so, must he not do so faithfully, leaving no stone unturned to see that the truth is transmitted in its entirety and received in meekness?

No one surely will desire that the hard-won beliefs and principles of bygone ages, which have passed through the crucible of time, should be lost. Who would advocate that each new batch of recruits to life's army should be obliged to work out anew the right principles of training? It is difficult to imagine that anyone will propose that each new entrant should start with a blank sheet of paper for a mind, on which nothing but the outcome of his own unaided and uninstructed experience is to be written? How will the world progress if that is to be the method? In reality of course there is no such thing as a continuously unaided and uninstructed experience: but the quality of the aid and instruction varies, not to mention the method!

On the other hand there is the right of the newcomer to a freely working mind. He must not be enslaved by any traditional views before he has had a chance to judge for himself. He should not be deprived of that most precious possession, a real personal conviction. Is any adult justified in imposing his creed upon the defenceless mind of his child or pupil? Is not he who does so guilty of warping that mind in such a way that it may never recover? The religious denomination which says "Give us the child young enough, and we will guarantee its loyalty to the Church ever afterwards" may well be regarded as treacherous to the cause of spiritual freedom and integrity.

The reply to this perplexing antinomy is plain enough in general terms, however difficult may be the application thereof. There is no escape from the duty of the adult to distribute what he regards as the best goods, to hand on those moral habits and judgments which have proved—or are believed to have proved—their worth, and not to withhold those thoughts about the universe which the insight of seers has revealed to men. In passing it might be added that it is difficult to see why he should be free to condemn evils which have long passed away, and debarred from exposing those which are still rampant in the earth.

It is an important truth that the moral standards to be effective have to be so ingrained as to act intuitively: they have to become part and parcel of the self, expressing themselves promptly as the natural reaction to the situation that arises. Burke, it may be, went too far in speaking of the disaster that would follow "if the practice of all moral duties and the foundations of society rested upon having their reasons made clear and demonstrative to every individual." But it is certain that the moral self in its hour to hour operation must function with the naturalness and promptitude of instinct. There is no escape from the necessity of training the young conscience: if the adult in charge does not play his part, habits of will and response will be formed nevertheless, whose quality will be a matter of hazard, and there is no reason to suppose that the child will be any the more self-legislative for his guardian's self-effacement. Other more questionable influences—from within or without—will have stepped in, far more dominating and warping than ever the deliberate educator would have been. By refusing to train the conscience, you will go far to ensure not its critical freedom, but its prejudiced enslavement.

It is extraordinarily wide of the mark to suppose that the absence of influence conduces to freedom.

It is broad views and developed sympathies that make for freedom and growth, and these seldom, if ever, come unaided. A new communicated idea that breaks down old barriers of ignorance and illuminates new tracts of thought may be as stimulating to mental activity as any self-directed investigations or unguided conclusions from experience.

Knowledge is both interest and power. A new fact or conception, if alive, is an instrument and an aspiration.

The point of doubt, if there is one, would appear to be whether the training in habits, the instilling of the ideals that lie at their back, and the inculcation of truths can be combined with the development of free judgment. No one will deny the difficulty, or doubt that there are many instructors of youth who do not succeed in doing this as fully as they should, though for my part I have never found the young so meek and docile as they are sometimes represented. But that these apparent opposites can be combined is fundamental. If they cannot, then education is an idle dream. It is in this very use of provided material and selected experience for the growth of the intelligence and character that education consists.

There is a notion not infrequently met with that this inevitable task can be escaped or its difficulty evaded by the simple presentation of facts, unaccompanied by any interpretation or instructive comment. This again is a dream, and a bad dream. You cannot enumerate all the facts of history, not even all the known facts, not let us hope all that you know yourself: at the very least you make a selection and order them on a certain plan. In proportion as you succeed in being colourless, you will be intolerably dull, all meaning will have vanished, and you will have failed to educate. In so far as you are in measure competent for your job, you will give forth facts, indicate, if only by your presentment of the case and the line of your questions, what is in your view their probable significance, and at the same time by your educative method kindle the desire for truth, and train the capacity for judgment. You will in fact leave the mind of your pupil, as in part the fruit of your tendance, able to turn upon itself, to bring its critical faculty into play, and to revise its opinions accordingly. Its future growth is the test of your success. The quality of self-directing, adventurous energy and initiative is no doubt of vital importance. But there are other desirable things too. What of humility and teachableness, the power of appreciation and reverence, the readiness to consider suggestions and criticisms?

The case, however, is less straightforward even in theory than would appear from this. In regard to morality, it is necessary as we have seen that the moral self should act almost automatically. How are we to build up something that shall act with unquestioned authority, while at the same time recognizing that the questioning faculty is to be encouraged? How can we seek to foster the prompt intuition of right, while admitting the claims of discussion? How is the passage to be made from a protectorate to autonomy and independence? Perhaps the certainty of drastic criticism to come

WHAT THEN OF EDUCATION?

is a reason for making early standards all the more secure: is that so?

I note that, writing of judgments of value in regard to sex and marriage, Hastings Rashdall says: "The dependence of these judgments upon an experience which cannot well be possessed by the young makes this department of morality peculiarly dependent in practice upon respect for moral authority."[1] In all spheres of conduct indeed, the fact that habits of moral action are a necessary foundation for the growth of moral discernment, is one of vital importance. Are we tending to overlook or underestimate it?

In the sphere of religious instruction, we ask how we are to teach without assuming and inculcating matters that are everywhere in dispute. It used to be a maxim that we should never teach anything that would have to be unlearned afterwards. There is much to be said for regarding this as an impossible ideal to-day, though the nearer we approximate to it the better.

In spite of all difficulties, it remains the duty of the educator to achieve so far as he can this seemingly impossible combination of incompatible things. The will and character must be turned and led in what seems to us the true direction. Education must have a deliberate ethical end in view: the educator (and this of course includes the parent, even the modern parent) cannot abdicate his duty

[1] *Theory of Good and Evil*, Oxford Press.

here. His task is to see to it that wider and fuller experience gives the help that it obviously should give, and then that the outward authority passes over to the inward, and the accepted law becomes the intelligible good. Ingrained morality, so far from being the inevitable enemy of the free moral judgment, is its essential condition. The solution of this transitional difficulty lies in part, on the disciplinary side, not in the abandonment of order and habit-making, but in the creation of a right relation between parents and children and between staff and pupils and in the growing share of the latter as they rise in the school, in the management of institutions, and the maintenance of community life. Freedom comes with influence that is assented to and understood. Broadly it is a question of making morality intelligent, and intelligence awake to the issues of morality.

On the instructional side, it is obvious that we cannot be shut up to a choice between unfair dictation and a refusal to influence. It is not a question of whether, but how. John Morley writes of John Stuart Mill, that he "appeals not to our sense of greatness and power in a teacher, which is noble, but to our love of finding and embracing truth for ourselves, which is still nobler. People who like their teacher to be as a king publishing decree with herald and trumpet, perhaps find Mr. Mill colourless. Yet this habitual effacement of his own personality marked a delicate and very rare shade in his reverence for the sacred purity of truth." Yet no one could say that Mill did not desire to persuade men to a certain line of thought. He was faithful alike to his duty to truth as he saw it and to the intellectual independence and integrity of his readers. Why indeed should man do otherwise? Truth is held by convincement, not by submission.

Moreover if the ethical aim is given its right place and the methods adopted are in accordance with the best educational principles, many of the religious difficulties will disappear. No one for whom the pre-eminent purpose is to aid the growth of a good twentieth-century Christian man and citizen will spend half a year in an uncritical teaching of the books of Joshua and Judges, or regard the belief in Elisha's miracles as essential. The one would be barbaric, and the other irrational and childish. Nor will any sound and thoughtful educator seek to instil doctrines and theories into a youthful mind without finding a basis for his instruction in facts which can be understood and appreciated, and experiences which have been felt and known. If true methods are being violated anywhere, it is where a Church imposes ready-made and abstruse doctrines upon helpless infants, and adopts the antiquated plan of a catechism learnt by heart.

Build upon simple inward facts, teach by stories and biographies which are of a nature to appeal but which stand broadly for an ethical purpose.

When deeper and more general truths come into view, introduce more and more the method of discussion. The difficulties presented by the Old Testament as a text-book of modern religious education have been discussed in an earlier chapter, but it may be worth while to stress again the importance of seeing it as a record whose value lies in its evolutionary character. Without this, early barbaric ideas receive a fresh sanction, and the anthropomorphic presentation of God's commands makes it difficult to show that they are superseded. How much is modern reluctance to admit the wickedness of war due to the prominence of the Old Testament and the pitifully irrational handling of its material, in the moral training of the young! If God is presented, beyond correction, as an external and separate being, whom you might meet when walking in the garden or in the wilderness, his utterances stand, and to transform these into "the notions of the men of that age" is not an easy task. Some recent discoveries of an early Canaanite civilization may help us to see the Israelitish conquest in its true light. We are not here flogging a dead horse. Large numbers of children are still being taught this in the words and spirit of the book of Joshua. To do so is as wrong as it would be to take an account of the Norman Conquest of England, written, say, by some fighting Norman Abbot, as the last word of historical and moral truth for the twentieth century.

Once more, to blend the recognition of the adult's duty with that of the child's autonomous rights is difficult, but essential. To the true educator this dual mandate will not be impossible. We are again in contact with our central theme: the problem is in part a question of valuing intelligence. We want live truth, not dead lumber; principles, not prejudices. The mind needs help in all stages of its growth, but it is help through increasing light to a developing life.

Neither here nor anywhere else, may I repeat, am I suggesting that intellectual aid alone will bring us the desired result. As a matter of fact, no mental process ever takes place without the presence of feeling, and of its place in the stirring, widening and fusing of character, much might be written. It is true that religion is life. We are not convinced by mere argument: the new thought needs time to make its attachments; it must be supported and sanctioned by the whole contents of the mind and character. Where the matters in question are intimately related to personal life, their entrance in genuine and living power will be largely dependent on the teacher's whole mental and moral attitude, his personality in short. As this embodies the vital truths which we desire that the pupil should grasp, they will come to him as real facts in the interrelated life of man. But they will only attain to a dominant, embracing and fruitful position, if they are consciously adopted as ideals.

Lastly, an education such as we have described demands a broad spirit of toleration, a belief in freedom for the teacher, a real understanding of what personal convictions are and of how valuable they are, and on the part of the teacher a strength and reality in his grasp of truth, coupled with a present sense of his own fallibility and an understanding of the meaning of progress for the individual and for humanity. If Reason is awake, how much of this will follow?

XV

A REASONABLE RELIGION

It is right that we should in conclusion try to gather together some of the scattered threads of our subject. A critical discussion of various conceptions of religion may have involved the presentation, from this point of view or that, of what was regarded as a better way. But the central questions remain: what after all is religion? Even if morality stands, is religion nothing more than another name for the same thing? What is left of its ancient claims, if reason is let loose upon it? If it requires an intellectual basis, what is that basis?

I think that the hope of religion lies, not in taking a completed conception and endeavouring to instil it into the minds of men, but in fastening upon indubitable facts in common human experience, approaching them with that power of valuation and integration with which the mind or soul is endowed, and so entering into possession of something of that spirit of all good which brings peace and power, and commands our humble worship and loyal service.

I refuse to believe that religion and the rational are antagonistic. I decline to leave rationalism to the anti-religious. Let us not be parties to handing over the claims of reason to be the property of those who see this power of the human spirit as something mainly destructive, as drily ratiocinative, as involving a mind shut up in a certain complacency of attitude with no open doors or windows, as limiting man's concern to the region of external relationships, as suspicious of all those fringes and depths of the inner life which may be its hope of purification and enlargement. Reason and inward sensitiveness and vision are close friends, if not indeed wedded in the one life. If religion is a matter of worship, reason will bring light and breadth; and in the thought about religion which it is difficult to separate from the practice of it, reason must be the guide that leads to truth. It is one of the activities of God.

There are those to whom the alleged facts and forces of religion have little or no reality. Those who speak of such things seem to them to have no foothold on the ground. The day to day doings and events of life we know, but as to these fine phrases or eloquent generalities, who are they? What need in any case is there of them? Life is a concrete series of deeds and happenings: high-sounding abstractions may be left to parsons and other moralists. Perhaps no one makes such an overt statement even to himself, but many tend to think and act that way, and all of us do at times. Yet to do so is to imagine that isolated details are everything, and the pattern they make nothing. It is as if you said that the real thing in a poem lay in the particular words considered as separate entities, or that in a sonata it was this and that sound, or this and that mark upon a page. Whereas we know that it is in the scheme, the meaning, the spirit, the unity of the whole, that the reality lives. So with life. It is the plan, the combined effect, the continuity of significance, the revelation of personality—it is these which count. This is not to say that details do not matter. They matter supremely. But if they were unrelated, they could not do so. They matter because they contribute to meaning and value. It may be also that some of the details which it is most important not to omit or slur over, are themselves neither seen nor heard nor measured. It looks then as though the unseen was important, the seen unimportant except in so far as it finds its ministering place in the unseen. To test the realities of religion we must take care not to miss inward facts, nor fail to appreciate the part played by meaning and value. Vision of inner phenomena first, then a synoptic view of the whole, and from these to the most satisfying interpretation we can reach.

Let us look for these inner facts,—or shall we say facts of experience on their inward side?—and try to name them without resort to any language of recognized religion. We know within ourselves a faculty of self-judgment. Indeed without any deliberate intention on our part, every act leaves its aftermath of approval or disapproval, and so "the dialectic of the soul" moves on. In the light of these judgments, we set purposes before us more or less consciously, purposes which are narrow and short-sighted, or comprehensive and far-seeing, as the case may be. In varying degree, we modify them as experience teaches or drives home its lessons. We live by standards,—inadequate, poor, self-contradictory perhaps, but still standards. We are not ready to take the advice of the cynic that we should make our standard as low as possible so as occasionally to enjoy the luxury of living up to it. We are really ordering our lives to some moral level. We review the past and envisage the future. An animal does not do this: a cow does not survey its conduct last week and resolve to act in similar or different fashion next week. We are perpetually criticizing the present self in the light of something beyond it. There is an interfering spirit of non-acquiescence—often choked, no doubt —which keeps us, or endeavours to keep us, on the move. We learn that some things bring us a greater measure of satisfaction or a deeper and more lasting satisfaction than others. We realize the meaning of our relationships with our fellows. We feel the inner consequences when we fall short or set the better things at nought. Our very failure and frustration presses upon us the existence of something higher, which both judges us and beckons us onward. To all there comes, even if less deep or frequent by reason of acquired hardness of heart, a warm response to the good. Courageous deeds, cheerfulness in desperate conditions, faithfulness in spite of all allurements, a following of some high call whatever the personal consequences—these things stir our hearts. There is a something there—present even when we have been following quite another course of life ourselves—which answers to the appeal. There is a greatness which is recognized as superior to all worldly standards of success, a beauty in tenderness and compassion better than all self-assertive strength. We feel even in a tragic fate such as closes the drama of King Lear, that in some sense there is victory. Within ourselves the sense of right insists upon being there: we cannot escape it. This and the power of ideals wherein it expresses itself may separate us from the stream of opinion, and lead to loneliness and suffering; but the call is imperative whatever the cost.

Occasions come to us from time to time when we are conscious that there are unrealized resources of power within us. Just as under the stimulus of overpowering fear a man can run or leap as he never knew he could, so if the spirit is roused there are moral achievements of self-conquest or devotion or purification which seemed impossible to the normal man, and which give, like the poet's or prophet's inspiration, the impression of being not ourselves. Just as the power of life which makes our muscles grow strong or our bodies gain healthy growth, is not in a sense ourselves, though it is we who do the exercises, so though we exert our wills and set our minds upon good, the power that comes is not something that we have made. We can seek it, we can enter into the condition which will bring it to us, but it comes. It is within us all the time; it is part of the true, potential self, but not of the known or realized self. It is spiritually transcendent. There is no ground for saying that this line of thought implies a worship of self which means complacency, stagnation, and hardness and dryness of heart: on the contrary, it is an assertion of an ineradicable element of restlessness, dissatisfaction with what is, and upreaching to what is better. It points to the pressure of a mighty reality, a reality that is objective and in some sense universal, but a pressure within the very precincts of the self. Where else could it be?

Should we not also agree that a measure of this added power comes into activity as we raise our desiring gaze in a teachable and seeking way to that which is within us but greater than we are? Or—if that sounds like an overstepping of the limits we have set to our phraseology—as we concentrate our thoughts, with intent to be the better for it, upon a level of life that is at the time beyond us? Let us make at this point what seems to me a fruitful comparison. Is not the action of this inward something not only analogous to that of friendship, but even more deeply akin to it? One who loves us, whether as an intimate friend or more closely still, sees beneath the surface to the real man, loves us for what we are potentially, has faith in that, and by his or her very confidence gives new power by which the possible becomes real. So too that which stirs within us refuses to lose hold of a faith in these latent capacities, and by this insistent and often disturbing expectation creates "the thing it contemplates."

I have described these things in a vague fashion, not because I want to imply religious meanings in surreptitious fashion, but because it is not here the exact psychological analysis that is important—though that could be given—but the net effect of the whole in regard to the values of life and the realization of them in the individual. You may explain this inner fact by reference to the central urge, particular instincts, the unifying and judging reason, the power of ideals, the finding and recognition of ultimate values in experience—by any of these or any combination of them. It is the upshot of it all that matters, and the fact remains that this power is part of man's endowment. The contents of the ideal man or higher self, as understood and consciously aimed at, will vary immensely, but the potency and direction are there: and however many the factors may appear to analysis, in their significant activity they are one.

We know too that as we enter upon this path and in any degree bring the whole complex and rebellious nature into line with it, we find a satisfaction, a freedom and a power, that is never won by following appetites, or impulses, "chance desires" that care nothing for the future or the balance and wholeness of life. All this means that our lives are set upon ends that are of intrinsic worth, supreme values; and these values mean personality. Nowhere else but in thinking and aspiring spirits can values live. And the same reason which seeks these values in itself, recognizes them in other men. Thus in so far as this recognition takes effect in the attitude of man to his own life and of man to man, he is the agent and recipient of the power of love. In love and knowledge we find our unity with other minds and with the outer world.

It is in facts such as these, which, even though the expression of them might vary, would for the most part be admitted as belonging to common human experience, that the stuff of religion consists; and although this suggests pre-eminently an inward view of religion, it is very far from being self-centred. Its eyes are upon life. Let anyone who can, take a step beyond this, or many steps, until the stuff takes coherent and appealing shape. Let him feel assured that the inward power, however many forms it may take and into whatever elements it may be dissected, is one, and that one a person in whose mind the supreme values have that objective existence which they can only have in a mind. Let him refuse to stop there, but feel the pressure of the unifying aim of reason to identify this spirit of life with the creator or sustainer of that universe which has produced the aspiring spirit of man as one of its most revealing fruits. I am not underestimating the import or what may be called the added human effectiveness, at least to many minds, of these enlarged conceptions; nor do I imagine that we can rest satisfied with a body of thought which ignores the riddles of the universe of space and time. "Beside the work of God which we have been tracing in the individual mind," says Professor Hocking, "there is a supplementary work of God in the world beyond the human will,—there at the origins of the plot which all events work out." But in this discussion I am concerned to emphasize that the substance of religion is there, undeveloped if you like, in such facts of immediate experience as have been indicated. And this, be it noted, is not the peculiar experience of exceptional people, described as mystics, but that of the ordinary mortal.

This line of thought will help to identify God with all the workings of good in the daily lives of men. So often we have had God on one side and all the strivings and aspirations, all the love and patience, all the beauty and tenderness of life on the other. It is essential to break this distinction down. Emphasize by all means the varying levels of life-quality, the coming of special times of illumination and power; show how the highest love will shed a new grace upon all the rest. But we must find God in the very texture of life. It is true that there may be a risk of His losing His distinguishing identity, as it were. Better this than that He should be isolated in the serenities of a distant heaven. Better that it should be difficult to locate Him in His presence amid the loves and fidelities of life than that we should set the love we owe Him over against them to the impoverishment and distortion of both. Rather feel Him vaguely in our personal responsibilities than shift the burden upon an alien power. Rather feel uncertain as to the sense in which personality can be attributed to Him, than so objectify Him in isolation that He has no constant place in the heart and conscience. It is seldom recognized that the main difficulty in acknowledging the personality of God is in the solitary character of the self. The division of one self-consciousness from another seems the most absolute gulf in the world. How can one personality be present in an infinite number of other personalities? This is a difficulty perhaps of the concrete imagination, whose limitations we have to recognize. If we believe in the unity and order of the world of fact, in the reality of supreme values, in the place of purpose in the explanation of things, in the existence of values and purposes only for and in conscious mind, and in personality as the highest and therefore the most revealing product of an evolving universe—personality which though so utterly individual seems at its best to overstep and transcend

A REASONABLE RELIGION

in a sense the separation from other personalities—then we shall face this problem with equanimity, each according to his need and his light.

In any case, if we thus base our position for practice and for theory upon verifiable experience, we have the foundations of a rational religion. I believe it is true that in the days to come we shall be obliged to be far more tolerant of varieties of interpretation of this experience than we have been in the past. The first thing needful is the mind that is sensitive on the inside; it is for the enlightened reason to take these inward facts, to see their significance, to enlarge their power, and to assign them their due place in life.

Does anyone say that this is to equate religion with mere morality? Why *mere* morality, I wonder? Is the good life so common or trivial a thing, that we dare to dismiss it as of small comparative account?

If the churches had been more ready to see religion and morality as one, their record would have been more creditable than it has been. If morality is regarded as a dry reluctant affair, stripped of all feeling, unconcerned with the depths of human nature, little better than enlightened self-interest or respectability, there may be warrant for consigning it to a lower grade. If it is a matter of rules and regulations, it will remain external and unattractive. If it is concerned with rewards and punishments, it knows nothing of the inherent satisfaction of the good and the natural hell of evil.

As a fact it is religion that has thus degraded morality. It is only a few generations ago that men were branded as heretics if not atheists for saying that virtue was its own reward. To be orthodox, you had to stress the motive of a future heaven. But if morality means the good life in the fullest and truest sense of the words, then it is at the very least the threshold of religion. In spite of all the ridicule cast upon it, there was much truth in Matthew Arnold's definition of religion as morality touched with emotion. The good is to be not only pursued dutifully, but loved devotedly. "Oh, how I love thy law." Add to this, though it can hardly be maintained that the true moral philosopher needs the addition, that religion asserts the real existence in some sense of ideal values—something more than mere subjective, individual notions—and you have the foundations of a spiritual view of the universe, and therefore the makings of religion. Let me quote a sentence from an article by Professor Gilbert Murray: "I trust for the general maintenance and gradual raising of the moral standard in a society such as ours: first to the influence of the facts of life and the lessons taught by experience; next to the social instincts and the reaction of a well-organized society upon its members by example, education and training, by liking and disliking, admiration and disapproval, and most of all to this inward Censor of whom the psychologists tell us, this inborn moral and aesthetic instinct, the ineradicable heritage of humanity, by which men have from the very beginning of civilization rejected and denied what they feel to be vile within them, sought what they love, and imitated what they admire." This is no narrow morality or humanism: it is an inward and spiritual approach to the supreme good. It may be true that morality stands for independence and religion for dependence. In so far as this is so, I suggest that it is because morality is the good life, and religion the means of attaining it. That is another reason for its close relation to education. But human goodness must always be growing, and for this there must be a sense of present inadequacy and need, and an attitude of reverence and seeking towards that which is above and beyond us. Any other would be self-satisfied and therefore not good.

Our religion is a religion of experience, and experience is our contact with reality. Moral values are part of the nature of things. The universe is a school of righteousness. To vary the metaphor, we have an anchor and a compass in our spiritual make-up. We are educable, and the world is such that we can be educated in it: in these two facts we have the heart of a spiritual and progressive conception of morals, religion and philosophy.

Religion and Reason have so much in common, that it would be strange if they should be found to be antagonists. Both seek for harmony and unity. Both refuse, or should refuse, to take a departmental view of life; for both a synoptic vision is essential. There is a sense in which all the higher reaches of the mind's activities are religious—the intellect as it aims at order, the imagination as it follows after beauty and understanding, the moral sense as it grows in breadth and depth and delicacy of perception.

In all we have the search for something stable and permanent, and we seek it because it is implicitly there at the heart of experience. We strive after an abiding self, a dedicated will, a controlled and purposeful life, a principle of obligation that transcends the momentary, an insight into intrinsic qualities and an understanding of their eternal worth beyond the vicissitudes of personal feeling or even personal existence, a sense of human values that involves the sanctity of the soul and the unity of mankind, a consciousness, it may be, that we are children of the universal life and reason and goodness. "Our scent for reality," says Professor Hocking, "our grip upon fact and value, are our experience of God as being thought with."

Thus far we have had chiefly in mind the facts of his own experience which the normal man can verify, and we have considered the important things to be that he should of course be alive to the experience in the first place, and then that he should appreciate the unity of its meaning, the greatness of its significance and the splendour of its summons. But this full grasp and understanding requires that he should fortify himself from the evidence of history and from the insight and contemplation of philosophy. If God is in men, He will be found in the story of the race. If He is not an external static judge, but an activity and a purpose, it may be that His presence will be more clearly traceable through the ages than in the experiences of a day. From no point of view can the aid of history be neglected. Here is our heritage, our opportunity for instruction in righteousness, our living picture of the developing education of humanity, our panorama of God in action on a large scale. What better test of the inmost spirit of the universe than the process by which man the pupil rises in the scale of being and learns the lessons of life! Whether we find the evidence in the general laws of conduct and its consequences, the tendencies of men and nations, their wider outlook, the emergence of spiritual criteria, the building up of good and the disintegration of evil, or (what is largely responsible for this) individually in the gleams of truth that have flashed into the minds of seers and thinkers, or divine conceptions of human living that have taken shape in the lives of the true leaders and saviours of mankind, in both respects the import of this line of thought for the interpretation of reality is patent. To the emphasis upon geniuses of the Spirit must be added the capacity of the generality of men, even though to begin with they reject and deride, eventually to appreciate and respond. Their vision was capable of expansion and is expanded.

There is nothing in our plea for experience or for reason to make us underestimate the personal and the historic. Experience needs history to inspire and instruct it; history must link itself with experience to become alive and significant. Reason will add light and strength by bringing in coherence.

What, for example, is the relation between the Jesus of History and the Spirit of Christ in the hearts of men? We use the term "Christ" very loosely and vaguely. This may be defended on the ground that man's need is an object of devotion, not exact definition. Nevertheless here as in other connections my case is for clarity as against confusion. If there is an available power for good, it will not be weakened by being understood. There is a constant need of a Socrates to cross-examine us as to the precise meaning we attach to these terms of religious phraseology. Is it sufficient in this case to note on the one hand that "that of God within us," or however we may express it, points us to the sanctity of the individual soul, the need of inner purity and sincerity, the brotherhood of man, the beauty and power of love and service, and on the other that these are the very things for which Jesus pre-eminently stood, and which his enduring influence sustains? Or do we seek for some more personal, even metaphysical, identification? Or do we prefer to dwell in the realm of religious imagery and put these questions by? One thing I would urge, and that is that this personal identification should never be made a point of theological insistence or supposed obligation.

The difficulty, if such it be, arises in some degree from a failure to distinguish between the inborn necessity and power of human spirit to reach upward to the good and to share in the universal life, and the contents of the spirit's thought which in part it wins by its play upon the facts of its own experience and in part receives with more or less understanding from that which others have won in the past. The Light Within is a personal endowment, but it is not independent of the historical fact that spiritual geniuses in bygone ages have seen and testified and lived. The God-part of us is not a supernatural and isolated department: it is all the good in us, inherited, learnt, felt, won. How much Jesus of Nazareth counts in this, each one of us knows best for himself, but it is unlikely that he knows it to its full extent.

Of the need of philosophy and the help that it can give, it is more difficult to speak. Many are inclined to fear it or to relegate it to a professional class of thinkers who appear to find some singular satisfaction therein. Yet they are very likely prepared to make glib theological assertions which involve knotty problems of metaphysics at every point. Or they say philosophy is beyond them: yet they read articles and books by modern physicists beside which even the *Critique of Pure Reason* is lucidity itself. After all, the author of the fourth Gospel was a philosopher. The fact is that most of us are philosophizing all the time, and the only question is what effort we are going to make to see that our philosophies are sound and deep. Stress simple experience as you like, lay all the desirable emphasis upon the attentive ear and the obedient will, and the problem of interpretation remains, and the need of the enlarged and unifying mind. The more the power of traditional belief and the habit of early regimentation decay, the more does any winning of a free and unified personality seem to involve some kind of philosophy. In practice the conscious part played by deliberate thought will vary no doubt from man to man. But it would be well if those who accept traditional statements simply and without question, or to whom religion is a matter of personal loyalty than which they want nothing better, could recognize the inspiration that may come in other ways. There is no single identical path to the higher life, though the refusal to think will never be a helpful guide. Even philosophic meditation and analysis may act as a quickening and kindling power to the soul.

"It is never to be forgotten," says Professor MacCunn, "that he who goes in search of a theory of his moral ideal travels by his own analytic path into a world of august and enduring objects. Is it to be wondered at if a man who has spent his deepest hours of meditation in the presence of Duty, of Public Good, and of the half-revealed and half-concealed possibilities of the individual life, and has habitually looked upon these facts with what Plato called "the eye of the soul," will be something more than the cold-blooded analyst in whom the world too often travesties the theorist? For in his own way he will have been led to see the vision, and as he muses in his silent and solitary hours, the fire will burn within him."[1]

Some will still feel that I am neglecting the fact that a man may think clearly but act badly, may see the better but follow the worse through weakness of will and bondage to appetite. No one can ignore this. It is a tragic truth, and the mutual influence of insight and action needs perpetual recognition and emphasis. We have been stressing insight, and will-power is by no means detached from clarity of vision. The understanding grasp of an ideal means strength. Others will say that I am relegating feeling, which seems to them the very essence of the religious mind, to an insignificant place in the recipe for life and growth. I think not. If you urge that the real thing in religion is to have a lowly and loving heart, I shall say no word against you beyond explaining again that my subject has been the intellect, reason, thought; that you cannot—and ought not to wish to—escape from that; that

[1] *The Making of Character*, Cambridge University Press.

the human spirit is one, and that love itself is not a mere emotion, but rather the feeling aspect of an understanding mind and of a purpose that stands the test of universality. It is, as William Watson said of song,

> the rose upon Truth's lips,
> the light in Wisdom's eyes.

The heart and the head are not two antagonistic organs; they are inseparable in the unity of the human soul.

"The objection to intellectualism," says Dean Inge, "loses its force if we use intelligence in the Platonic sense, not of the logic-chopping faculty, but of the whole personality become self-conscious and self-directing, under the guidance of its highest part.... The spiritual life is or should be a harmonious development of the whole man, passing, as Clement of Alexandria says, from faith to knowledge, and from knowledge to that love which 'unifies the knower and the known.' In this state of enlightenment there is no more discord between the will, the intellect, and the feelings; and the objects of our reverence—the True, the Beautiful and the Right—are more and more blended, like a triple star."[1]

[1] *Science, Religion and Reality,* Edited by Joseph Needham, Sheldon Press.

INDEX

Adam and Eve, 106, 123
Æschylus, 62
Alexander, S., 40
Alfred the Great, 65
Arnold, Matthew, 58, 172

Baptism, 88
Beethoven, 62, 103
Behaviourism, 94
Bentham, 132
Bergson, 34
Bethlehem, 80
Bible, 18, 26, 30
Biblical Criticism, 76, 79
Bradley, F. H., 132
Bright, John, 66
Bruno, Giordano, 66
Butler, Bishop, 132

Catholic, Roman, 89
Chicago, 91
Christ, 12, 13, 27, 28, 55, 87, 109, 132, 176
Christian Science, 86, 91
Churches, 15, 57, 80, 81, 84, 119, 132, 140, 157
Clement of Alexandria, 180
Collingwood, R. G., 58, 59, 74, 111
Columbus, 66
Communion Service, 116
Creeds, 57, 80

Daniel, 106
Darwin, 22
Deuteronomy, 120

Eddington, 129
Einstein, 103
Elisha, 157
Euripides, 65
Evangelicals, 91
Evolution, 12, 33

Feeling, 44, 130, 180
Fisher, H. A. L., 87
Forgiveness, 141
Francis of Assisi, 65
Friends, Society of, 52, 117

Galileo, 22
Galloway, 44
Galsworthy, 125
Gambling, 124
Garibaldi, 24
Garnett, Campbell, 96
Genesis, 15
Gresham's Law, 92
Guidance, 50

Head and heart, 16, 180
Hebrews, 26, 63, 64
Herod, 81
Hobhouse, L. T., 31
Hocking, W. E., 60, 97, 135, 169, 174
Holy Spirit, 13, 108
Hume, 40
Hyde, Lawrence, 58, 60

Inge, Dean, 180
Instinct, 12, 95, 135
Israel, 26, 64, 158

Italy, 24

James, 63
Jeans, 129
Jehovah, 27
Jericho, 64
Jesus, 24, 25, 30, 76, 106, 113, 141, 176, 177
Joseph, 81
Joshua, 157, 158
Judges, 157

Kant, 145
Keats, 62
Kepler, 129
King Lear, 165

Lecky, 129
Light Within, 177
Lippmann, 126
Luther, 22
Lying, 124

MacCunn, 178
Marriage, 48, 134, 155
Mill, J. S., 156
Moffatt, 141
Morley, 77, 156
Moses, 120
Murray, Gilbert, 172

Nansen, 103
Nazareth, 19, 80, 81
Newton, 19, 129

Old Testament, 26, 27, 58, 158

Paul, 63, 107

Penal methods, 140
Plato, 40, 55, 65, 132, 147, 179
Protestantism, 22
Psalms, 58
Ptolemy, 19, 129

Rashdall, 129, 155
Resurrection, 107
Revelation, 106
Rousseau, 22

Sacraments, 12, 114
Salvation Army, 91
Science, 39, 60, 75
Second Coming, 87
Self-sacrifice, 141
Sex, 94, 95, 135–9, 155
Socrates, 65, 176
Stoics, 62
Sunday, 144

Taylor, A. E., 90
Temple, Dr., 59
Turner, J. E., 33
Tyrrell, George, 118

Unconscious, 49, 98
Universal (and Particular), 22, 37, 104

Virgin birth, 15, 106

War, 27, 86, 140
Washington, George, 22
Watson, William, 180
Wesleyanism, 91
White, Douglas, 139
Whitehead, A. N., 45, 111
Woolman, John, 66

For Product Safety Concerns and Information please contact our EU
representative GPSR@taylorandfrancis.com
Taylor & Francis Verlag GmbH, Kaufingerstraße 24, 80331 München, Germany

www.ingramcontent.com/pod-product-compliance
Lightning Source LLC
Chambersburg PA
CBHW061448300426
44114CB00014B/1892